W9-DIN-846

Instructor's Guide

for

THE INTERPERSONAL COMMUNICATION VIDEO

Thomas E. Jewell and Jean Civikly-Powell
University of New Mexico

to accompany

Joseph A. DeVito

THE INTERPERSONAL COMMUNICATION BOOK

Eighth Edition

 LONGMAN

An imprint of Addison Wesley Longman, Inc.

New York • Reading, Massachusetts • Menlo Park, California • Harlow, England
Don Mills, Ontario • Sydney • Mexico City • Madrid • Amsterdam

Instructor's Guide for THE INTERPERSONAL COMMUNICATIONS VIDEO to accompany
DeVito, THE INTERPERSONAL COMMUNICATIONS BOOK, Eighth Edition

Copyright © 1997 Longman Publishers USA, A Division of Addison Wesley Longman, Inc.

All rights reserved. Printed in the United States of America. No part of this book may be used or
reproduced in any manner whatsoever without written permission from the publisher except,
testing materials may be copied for classroom use. For information, address Addison Wesley
Educational Publishers Inc., 10 East 53rd Street, New York, NY 10022.

ISBN: 0-321-00404-3

12345678910 - CB - 00999897

TABLE OF CONTENTS

VIDEO 1: "MARY POPPINS"--INTERPERSONAL PERCEPTION (8:48) 1

SCRIPT 3
RELATED CONCEPTS 11
QUESTIONS FOR CLASS DISCUSSION 12
EXERCISE 1: WHO'S WHO 13
EXERCISE 2: INTERPRETING INTERPERSONAL BEHAVIOR ATTRIBUTIONS 14
ADDITIONAL RESOURCES 15
OTHER REFERENCES ON INTERPERSONAL PERCEPTION 16

VIDEO 2: "NOT EXACTLY"--ETHICS/LYING (3:40) 17

SCRIPT 19
RELATED CONCEPTS 24
QUESTIONS FOR CLASS DISCUSSION 25
EXERCISE 1: A LYING INVENTORY 26
EXERCISE 2: EXPLORING LYING ON THE WORLD WIDE WEB 28
ADDITIONAL RESOURCES 29
OTHER REFERENCES ON LYING 30

VIDEO 3: RAISED BY WOLVES--SELF-DISCLOSURE (6:10) 31

SCRIPT 33
RELATED CONCEPTS 39
QUESTIONS FOR CLASS DISCUSSION 40
EXERCISE 1: ANALYZING SELF-DISCLOSURES 41
EXERCISE 2: THE BREAKFAST CLUB 42
ADDITIONAL RESOURCES 43
OTHER REFERENCES ON SELF-DISCLOSURE 44

VIDEO 4: "CHECK, PLEASE"--APPREHENSION AND ASSERTIVENESS (6:00) 45

SCRIPT 47
RELATED CONCEPTS 54
QUESTIONS FOR CLASS DISCUSSION 55
EXERCISE 1: AN ASSERTIVENESS DIARY 56
EXERCISE 2: PRACTICING ASSERTIVE BEHAVIOR 57
ADDITIONAL RESOURCES 58
OTHER REFERENCES ON APPREHENSION AND ASSERTIVENESS 59

VIDEO 5: "PSA #136"--VERBAL PITFALLS (3:30).. **61**

SCRIPT 63
RELATED CONCEPTS 67
QUESTIONS FOR CLASS DISCUSSION 68
EXERCISE 1: ARE YOU BRISTLING? 69
EXERCISE 2: OBSERVING SOCIAL GROUP INTERACTIONS 70
ADDITIONAL RESOURCES 71
OTHER REFERENCES ON VERBAL PITFALLS 72

VIDEO 6: "SIX MONTHS IN"--CONVERSATIONAL MANAGEMENT (6:45).............. **73**

SCRIPT 75
RELATED CONCEPTS 83
QUESTIONS FOR CLASS DISCUSSION 84
EXERCISE 1: GOOD TALKER? GOOD LISTENER? 85
EXERCISE 2: SCRIPT ANALYSIS 86
ADDITIONAL RESOURCES 87
OTHER REFERENCES ON CONVERSATIONAL MANAGEMENT 88

VIDEO 7: "RENT"--SEXUAL HARASSMENT (7:31)... **89**

SCRIPT 91
RELATED CONCEPTS 99
QUESTIONS FOR CLASS DISCUSSION 100
EXERCISE 1: PRACTICE SAYING "NO"! 101
EXERCISE 2: SEXUAL HARASSMENT RESOURCES ON THE WEB 102
ADDITIONAL RESOURCES 103
OTHER REFERENCES ON SEXUAL HARASSMENT 104

VIDEO 8: "ONE MORE CHANCE"--DYSFUNCTIONAL RELATIONSHIPS (4:36) .. **107**

SCRIPT 109
RELATED CONCEPTS 115
QUESTIONS FOR CLASS DISCUSSION 116
EXERCISE 1: SCRIPT ANALYSIS 117
EXERCISE 2: COMMUNICATING THROUGH SCRIPT WRITING AND ACTING 118
ADDITIONAL RESOURCES 119
OTHER REFERENCES ON DYSFUNCTIONAL RELATIONSHIPS 120

ACKNOWLEDGMENTS

The videotape of the eight interpersonal communication scenarios is the result of countless hours of work by ten undergraduate students at the University of New Mexico who spent countless hours on this project.

We also want to thank Dax, Darci, Joe, and Richard of Sunrise Studios for their friendly and professional work on the production of the video.

All Script Creations: Jessica Clark

SCRIPT	ACTORS
Mary Poppins	Anna M. Soule Howard L. Kaibel III
Not Exactly	Shenita King Sarah E. Myers
Raised by Wolves	Anna M. Soule Joshua Jevon Narcisso
Check, Please!	hushari Jayasekara Shenita King Victoria Regina Gonzales
PSA #136	Tasha Martin Thushari Jayasekara Joshua Jevon Nascisso
Six Months In	Victoria Regina Gonzales Joshua Jevon Narcisso
Rent	Charmaine Rae Jackson Prof. Tom Jewell
One More Chance	Erin Foy-Stewart Joshua Jevon Narcisso

Incorporating Videos In Class Instruction

This instructor's video guidebook is designed to provide instructors with suggestions for ways to use the video scenarios as part of class instruction. Materials provided in the guidebook for each scenario include

- The script for the scenario

- A key to concepts in the textbook, identified as <u>primary concepts</u> that deal directly with the scene and <u>secondary concepts</u> that can be discussed as part of the larger communication picture.

- A list of questions about the videotape that can be used to stimulate class discussion

- Two exercises designed to highlight concepts from the textbook and relate these to the video segment

- A list of additional resources that instructors may want to review or have students review as part of a class assignment

- A list of references on each of the content areas

Here are several suggestions of ways to incorporate the video segments in class instruction:

- Have the students view the video scenario during class. After viewing, use the questions provided in this guidebook to conduct a class discussion with the class at-large, or divide students into small groups and assign each group a question for them to discuss and then to report to the class.

- Have the students view the video scenario during class. After viewing, distribute copies of the in-class exercises that are provided in this guidebook. Exercises may also be part of the course's graded assignments or may be used as "extra-credit" assignments.

- Students may do more extended research on any of the video topics and can begin by using references provided in this guidebook.

- The video segments may be assigned for viewing and analysis to students who are absent from class, with directions to complete questions and/or exercises that accompany the video segment.

- The video segments may be used as a focus for test questions. The questions may be any form of objective questions and/or a critical essay question.

Mary Poppins

INTERPERSONAL PERCEPTION

"MARY POPPINS"

A free clinic decorated minimally. It's nearly Thanksgiving. MARY sits in the waiting room. She is a woman in her mid twenties, dressed in a white sweater and flower print skirt. She has a backpack. She has a cigarette in her hand which she taps against the empty chair next to her. She shifts in her seat, leafs through a magazine, etc. DREW, a man in his early twenties, sits a row behind her and a few seats away from her. He is wearing jeans and a tight shirt. His hair is cropped short and he is wearing two silver earrings. DREW is watching MARY intently but is interrupted briefly as he whistles at a passerby.

DREW

'Scuse me! 'Scuse me buns of steel? Would you come over here please! *(pauses, then to MARY)* You gonna smoke that?

MARY

Excuse me?

DREW

You going to smoke that cigarette?

MARY

I was thinking about it.

DREW

You've been tapping it against that chair for about twenty minutes now. When do you think you'll decide?

MARY

Am I bothering you?

DREW

No -- it's just odd. Most smokers smoke as soon as they get the urge, you know.

MARY

Oh, I'm not really a smoker. I just smoke when I'm nervous . . .

DREW

Or when frat boy Biff buys you too many wine coolers?

MARY

I don't smoke all the time.

DREW

I didn't think so.

MARY

Do you want the damn cigarette?

DREW

I usually don't smoke cigarettes with flowers printed on the filter.

MARY

Fine.

DREW

But, if you're not going to smoke it. You know you probably shouldn't be smoking if you're pregnant anyway.

MARY

What?

DREW

It's bad for the baby. I mean, you may not want it but . . .

MARY

I'm not . . . What are you talking about?

DREW

Calm down. I'm not going to tell your parents.

MARY

Do you enjoy being so hostile towards people you don't know?

DREW

Sorry. I just get so sick of people like you coming in here -- scared that your world is going to come crashing down because you skipped a period or whatever.

MARY

What time is it?

DREW

Four, give or take a few minutes.

She lights the cigarette, and immediately chokes. Drew laughs.

DREW

Careful.

MARY

Do they usually start this late? This is unbearable. They could at least start on time. Isn't it supposed to start at four?

DREW

The HIV results start at four, yeah.

MARY

Aren't you nervous?

DREW

Should I be?

MARY

It's like a life and death situation. I'm pretty nervous. I'm completely terrified.

DREW

And you just assume I'm in here for an AIDS test?

MARY

Aren't you?

DREW

Because I'm a fag?

MARY

That's not what I meant.

DREW

Sure it is.

MARY

I just assumed. Why else? I'm sorry.

DREW

All us gay guys in the high risk group who meet strangers at the club and have wild criminal flings. And I should be scared -- you'd be scare if you were me. But thank goodness you're not. Thank goodness you're just here because Biff slept with one of those Alpha Beta Gamma girls while you were at your grandmother's funeral in July.

MARY

I don't even have a boyfriend.

DREW

You're here because you just found out that your boyfriend from high school slept with the quarterback so you had to run and get tested.

MARY

Stop it! Just stop it. I'm sorry I broke in on your private club. How dare I come into your neighborhood clinic.

DREW

And I should be so privileged to be a member. You too can be a member for only $19.95 and proof that you too have the HIV virus. Included with your official membership card is weekly visits to this luxurious clinic for AZT treatments, and if you act now you can even get a pre-planned funeral package with your choice of oak, mahogany, or pine casket.

There is a long, uncomfortable pause.

MARY

I didn't realize.

DREW

Most people don't.

MARY

How long?

DREW

How long have I had it or how long do I have to live?

MARY

The first.

DREW

About a year.

An awkward pause. Neither knows exactly what to say.

MARY

Are you sick?

DREW

Not yet.

MARY

Well how did you tell your parents? Do your parents know?

DREW

Yeah.

MARY

How did you tell them?

DREW

I just told them. What do you mean?

MARY

I mean how did you bring it up? I don't know how I'm -- how I would tell my parents. That's my biggest worry. They think I'm so -- Mary Poppins, ya know?

DREW

You'd be surprised.

MARY

I don't think they'll ever speak to me again.

DREW

(moves over to the seat next to MARY) Hey, you don't have anything to worry about, okay? The chances are so small -- very small. Okay?

MARY

You don't know what I've done.

DREW

Look, they're very small. What'd you do, sleep with a guy at a party in 1993?

MARY

A few times.

DREW

That's still really low risk.

MARY

I did more than that.

DREW

Look, don't worry about it. You're gonna be okay -- what's your name?

MARY

Mary.

DREW

Drew. What's your number?

MARY

415.

DREW

Relax.

MARY

I can't.

  DREW

Think happy thoughts.

                                          MARY

In a mocking tone. Like ice cream and Christmas!

                                          DREW

Like Chris O'Donnell.

                                          MARY

Chris O'Donnell. . . . Like I'm not HIV positive.

                                          DREW

Well, even if you are, it's not the end of the world.

                                          MARY

Really?

                                          DREW

Really.

                                          MARY

When your parents -- when you told your parents -- what did they do?

                                          DREW

Nothing. They pretend not to know. I pretend not to care. They send me Christmas presents. I
skip the "home for the holidays" trip.

                                          MARY

I'm sorry.

                                          DREW

You say that a lot. Don't be. I'm not.

                                          MARY

She takes off her sweater. 409.
She pulls up her sleeves, revealing faded needle marks. Drew notices and looks away.

                                          DREW

Happy thoughts!

                                          MARY

But what if I . . . ?

                                          DREW

The chances are very small -- very, very, small.

                                MARY

If you only knew.

                                DREW

What?

                                MARY

I used to get so lonely.

                                DREW

We all get lonely -- no matter who we sleep with -- or what our SAT scores are -- or, *(he touches her arm)* what we shoot up our veins -- it's life.

                                MARY

Wow - that's me. *She gets up to get her test results.*

                                DREW

I'll be right here.

                                MARY

Okay.

She remains standing there.

                                DREW

Well, what are you waiting for?

                                MARY

Okay.

She exits.

                                DREW

Good luck.

He takes a deep breath and takes a drag from her cigarette. He begins tapping it against the chair and shifts nervously, much like Mary was earlier. Mary returns with a piece of paper clasped in her hand.

                                MARY

I can't look. . . . Will you?

                                DREW

Are you sure? *She nods her head.* Okay. *He unfolds the piece of paper, lets out a sigh, and smiles.* I'm sorry. You don't qualify for a membership today.

MARY

It's negative?

DREW

Yes.

MARY

Oh, thank you God! Thank you, thank you, thank you. I've never been so relieved. I've never been so happy. *She realizes she is celebrating alone. She looks at Drew.* I . . . uh . . .

DREW

It's okay. I'm happy for you.

MARY

Well, I have to go. . . . Uh, it was really nice meeting you.

DREW

It was nice meeting you too.

MARY

Thanks for -- um, thanks for being here for me.

DREW

Hey look, you gotta go. You're going to be late. This place is really depressing.

MARY

You can have these - *she hands him her cigarettes.* Good-bye Drew.

DREW

Bye Mary.
Mary begins to exit. Drew stays in the waiting room and lights his cigarette. Before she reaches the door she turns around.

MARY

Drew?

DREW

Yeah?

MARY

What are you doing for Thanksgiving?

-END OF SCENE-

"MARY POPPINS" - INTERPERSONAL PERCEPTION

Related Concepts in *THE INTERPERSONAL COMMUNICATION BOOK*

Primary Concepts: Unit 6: Perception in Interpersonal Communication

Sensory Stimulation
Attributions and Errors
The Self-Serving Bias
Perception Checking
Implicit Personality Theory
Stereotyping
Uncertainty Reduction Strategies
Increasing Interpersonal Perception Accuracy

Other Concepts: **Unit 2: Axioms of Interpersonal Communication**
Unit 4: The Self in Interpersonal Communication
Unit 13: Nonverbal Messages: Space and Time
Unit 15: Universals of Interpersonal Relationships

Interpersonal Communication is a Transactional Process
Communication in Inevitable, Irreversible, and Unrepeatable
Communication Accommodation
Interpersonal Communications Have Content and Relationship Dimensions
Self-esteem
Factors Influencing Self-Disclosure
Rewards of Self-Disclosure
Clothing and Body Adornment
Stages in Interpersonal Relationships

Questions about "Mary Poppins"

1. What examples of interpersonal perception did you notice in the opening minutes of this scenario? Examples of how Mary perceived Drew? Examples of how Drew perceived Mary?

2. What stimuli contributed to those interpersonal perceptions (attire, cigarette tapping, Drew's call to a passerby, language "frat boy Biff," vocal cues, the setting, etc.)?

3. How were attributions (reasons for why a person behaves a certain way) evident in this scenario? Did you see any self-serving bias operating?

4. Laing describes interpersonal communication as the ongoing exchange of experiences and perceptions. It is the result of the way two people perceive themselves, perceive each other, and how each thinks the other perceives him/her. How would you describe Mary's and Drew's perceptions of self, of each other, and of how each thinks the other perceives her/him?

5. How did Mary's perception of Drew change during their encounter? How did Drew's perception of Mary change during their encounter (related to primacy and recency effects)?

6. What are some examples of how Mary and Drew engaged in perception checking?

7. Why do you think this scenario is titled "Mary Poppins?" What would you title it?

Other examples and experiences of differing perceptions:
- how political leaders are perceived differently (president, state leaders, city leaders, organizational leaders)
- how media personalities are perceived differently (Madonna, Howard Stern, David Letterman, Rush Limbaugh, Kathie Lee Gifford, Jim Carrey)
- how community activists are perceived differently
- how sports figures, teams, and referees are perceived differently

Exercise 1: Who's Who

Distribute blank half-sheets of paper to your students with instructions that they write down 5 characteristics of self that are not immediately evident to others, e.g., a car you might like to own, what you would do to relax, etc. Collect the papers and read each list to the class. See if students can identify the owners, and more importantly, discuss why certain descriptions were attributed to certain individuals. Ask students to discuss how the results relate to interpersonal perceptions, attributions, and expectations.

Exercise 2: Interpreting Interpersonal Behavior/Attributions

In perceiving and interpreting another person's behaviors, we often take certain conditions into consideration, e.g., such as how well we know the other person, how the person looks, etc. For eachof the the following considerations, comment on how you interpret Drew's behaviors and how you interpret Mary's behaviors. Do these circumstances affect how you attribute meaning to their behaviors?

Considerations Influencing Attributions

DREW

1. intentionality of the person's behavior
2. external factors affecting the person's behavior
3. the person's internal state (mental, emotional)
4. how the person's behavior is labeled (use of language)
5. characteristics of the person (age, gender, sexual orientation, education, socio-economic status, ethnicity, etc.)
6. the person's skills and abilities
7. the person's values and beliefs
8. provocations made to the person about the behavior (free choice? forced?)
9. habits and past experiences of the person that pertain to the behavior

MARY

1. intentionality of the person's behavior
2. external factors affecting the person's behaviors
3. the person's internal state (mental, emotional)
4. how the person's behavior is labeled (use of language)
5. characteristics of the person (age, gender, sexual orientation, education, socio-economic status, ethnicity, etc.)
6. the person's skills and abilities
7. the person's values and beliefs
8. provocations made to the person about the behavior (free choice? forced?)
9. habits and past experiences of the person that pertain to the behavior

Additional Resources

Osgood, Charles (1981*). *There is Nothing That I Wouldn't Do If You Would Be My POSSLQ**.
"The Difference Between You and Me." New York: Holt, Rinehart & Winston. 32-33.
*(People of opposite sex sharing living quarters")

Two stanzas from this poem suggest its theme and message:

> When it's you reading some periodical
> Sitting back on some comfortable perch
> It's a waste, whereas I'm so methodical
> That it goes by the name of research. . . .
>
> You are nosy and I am observant.
> The events of the day have me shook.
> I'm a wonderful national servant.
> While you, I suspect, are a crook.

Comic Strips on Relationships, e.g., *CATHY* by Cathy Guisewite, Universal Press Syndicate.

John Godfrey Saxe, "The Parable of the Blind Men and the Elephant."

"The Breakfast Club." A John Hughes film. An A&M Film Channel Production, 1985.

Jerzy Kosinski (1970), *Being There*, Bantam Books. Also *Being There* (1979), A North Star International Picture, Lorimar Distribution International, United Artists Release.

Other References on Interpersonal Perception

Donohue, William A. with Robert Kolt (1992). Face Saving. In *Managing Interpersonal Conflict*, pp. 48-66, Newbury Park, California: Sage.

Fein, Steven (1996). Effects of Suspicion on Attributional Thinking and the Correspondence Bias. *Journal of Personality and Social Psychology* 70 (June):1164-1184.

Goffman, Erving (1959). *The Presentation of Self in Everyday Life*. New York: Garden City, Doubleday Anchor.

Gray, John (1992). *Men are from Mars, Women are from Venus*. New York: HarperCollins.

Hinton, Perry (1993). *The Psychology of Interpersonal Perception*. New York: Routledge.

Jones, Edward E. (1990). *Interpersonal Perception*. New York: W.H. Freeman.

Kenny, David A. (1994). *Interpersonal Perception: A Social Relations Analysis*. New York: Guilford.

Laing, Ronald D., Herbert Phillipson and A. Russell Lee (1966). *Interpersonal Perception: A Theory and a Method of Research*. New York: Spring Publishing.

Lee, Fiona, Mark Hallahan and Thaddeus Herzog (1996). Explaining Real-life Events: How Culture and Domain Shape Attributions. *Personality and Social Psychology Bulletin* 22 (7):732-741.

McDonnell, James R. (1993). Judgments of Personal Responsibility for HIV Infection: An Attributional Analysis. *Social Work* 38 (July):403-410.

Quigley, Brian M. and James T. Tedeschi (1996). Mediating Effects of Blame Attribution on Feelings of Anger. *Personality and Social Psychology Bulletin* 22 (December)1280-1288.

Schneider, David J., Albert H. Hastorf and Phoebe C. Ellsworth (1979). *Person Perception*, 2nd ed., Reading, Massachusetts: Addison-Wesley.

Stewart, Robert A., Graham E. Powell and Jane Chetwynd (1979). *Person Perception and Stereotyping*. Franborough, England: Saxon House.

Not Exactly

ETHICS/LYING

"NOT EXACTLY"

Sarah is applying make-up in the mirror. Shenita sits on the couch, thumbing though a magazine.

SHENITA

I am so excited for you! Do you know how incredible this is? I mean, do you realize how long I've listened to you go on and on about this guy? A long time.

SARAH

Believe me, I'm aware of how long I've been hung up on him. I'm the one who's been sleeping alone.

SHENITA

Sarah!

SARAH

It's too true. I can't believe it's actually happening.

SHENITA

Well, you deserve it.

SARAH

Do I look okay?

SHENITA

Your lipstick is not even.

SARAH

I'm so nervous -- I'm shaking. Look at this. I'm literally shaking.

SHENITA

Calm down. You'll be fine.

SARAH

I'm sure I'll be fine. It's Patrick I'm worried about. Poor thing - bored out of his mind because I can't open my mouth. Does this top look okay? Does it make me look fat?

SHENITA

You look great.

SARAH

Did the other shirt look better?

SHENITA

They both looked great. You look great.

SARAH

I'm going to change.

SHENITA

You know, you really don't have anything to worry about. The hard part is already over. You asked him out -- and he said yes. He actually said yes. It's smooth sailing from here on in.

SARAH

I never could have done that without you.

SHENITA

That is so not true.

SARAH

Really. If you hadn't found that he was interested in me. You laid the trap, I just picked it up after the catch was made. Does this look better?

SHENITA

I told you -- you look great.

SARAH

You keep saying that. I just want to know what looks the best.

SHENITA

Honestly -- both look equally great.

SARAH

Could you honestly just tell me what you would wear?

SHENITA

I would wear that shirt.

SARAH

Really?

SHENITA

I'm just being honest.

SARAH

Okay. You know what I'm worried about most? I don't have a thing to say to him. Thank God he liked my presentation -- that gives me something to go on.

                    SHENITA

He liked your presentation?

                    SARAH

Didn't he?

                    SHENITA

The Heidegger presentation?

                    SARAH

That's what he told you, right?

                    SHENITA

Oh -- right.

                    SARAH

That's the whole reason I asked him out. That and you said he said he was really interested in me.

                    SHENITA

Sarah . . .

                    SARAH

How's this? Wow. I feel great. I can't wait. What time is it?

                    SHENITA

Sarah, Patrick didn't really like your Heidegger presentation.

                    SARAH

What?

                    SHENITA

In fact he hated it.

                    SARAH

But you said . . .

                    SHENITA

I know what I said -- look, I don't want you to freak out -- but I also don't want you rattling away about Being and Time or whatever.

                    SARAH

You said that he loved my presentation and that's how I came up in conversation.

                    SHENITA

That is how you came up in conversation.

                    21

SARAH

Oh. He said, "I hated Sarah's presentation," and you said, "Really, that's funny because she's obsessed with you," and he said, "Great, she should ask me out"?

SHENITA

He said, "I hate Heidegger. He's a Nazi," and I said, "Sarah gets on strange kicks," and he said you were very interesting.

SARAH

What?

SHENITA

He did say you were very interesting.

SARAH

But not that I should ask him out!

SHENITA

He said yes.

SARAH

Yes, but . . .

SHENITA

But what?

SARAH

I'm not going.

SHENITA

Sarah -- so he hates Heidegger and he didn't tell me to tell you to ask him out -- but he is going out with you -- he is interested. Why don't you let him give you a chance?

SARAH

I can't believe you lied to me.

SHENITA

I didn't lie. I encouraged you. Because I knew you wouldn't do it on your own.

SARAH

You're right about that.

SHENITA

Come on. Pull yourself together -- he's going to be here any minute.

SARAH

I am glad you manipulated me into this.

SHENITA

So am I. Now maybe I won't have to listen to you babble about him constantly!

SARAH

If all goes well.

SHENITA

It will. Now, let's fix your lipstick.

SARAH

So. I won't mention Heidegger. What should I talk about?

SHENITA

Well, he's a music major....

-END OF SCENE-

"NOT EXACTLY"—ETHICS/LYING

Related Concepts in *THE INTERPERSONAL COMMUNICATION BOOK*

Primary Concepts: Unit 1: Universals of Interpersonal Communication
  Unit 9: Universals of Verbal and Nonverbal Messages

Interpersonal Ethics: Interpersonal Ethics and Choice
Interpersonal Ethics: Lying

Other Concepts: Unit 2: Axioms of Interpersonal Communication
  Unit 4: The Self in Interpersonal Communication
  Unit 8: Effectiveness in Interpersonal Communication
  Unit 9: Universals of Verbal and Nonverbal Messages
  Unit 10: Verbal Messages: Principles and Pitfalls
  Unit 12: Nonverbal Messages: Body and Sound

Communication is Inevitable, Irreversible, and Unrepeatable
Self-Concept
Self-Awareness
Self-Esteem
A Humanistic Model of Interpersonal Effectiveness
  Openness
  Supportiveness
  Positiveness
  Equality
Meanings and Messages
  Meanings Are More Than Words and Gestures
  Meanings Are Context Based
Message Characteristics
  Messages Are Packaged
  Messages Vary in Believability
  Fact-Inference Confusion
  Facial Communication
  Eye Communication

Questions about "Not Exactly"

1. Was Shenita lying when she told Sarah that Patrick liked her Heidegger presentation?

2. Why do you think Shenita told Sarah that Patrick liked her Heidegger presentation? Does her reason make sense?

3. Does it matter if the results of Shenita's lie were positive? Why or why not?

4. Was Shenita's lie <u>ethical</u>? Why or why not?

Other Questions About Lying and Ethics

1. Under what circumstances do you consider lying acceptable in interpersonal situations?

2. What factors about one person talking to another might influence if and how a person might lie (e.g., age, relationship, like-dislike, anger, stress, etc.)?

Exercise 1: A Lying Inventory

Do not put your name on this inventory, but bring it to class to turn in to your instructor. answer the following questions by placing an "X" in the space that comes closest to representing your attitude about lying.

1=strongly disagree 2=disagree 3=neither disagree nor agree 4=agree 5=strongly agree

	1 sd	2 d	3 n d/a	4 a	5 sa
1. Lying is never acceptable.	—	—	—	—	—
2. Small lies are acceptable but large lies aren't.	—	—	—	—	—
3. Lying is worse than stealing.	—	—	—	—	—
4. Lying is natural.	—	—	—	—	—
5. Liars are easy to detect.	—	—	—	—	—
6. Most people lie occasionally.	—	—	—	—	—
7. I don't like it when people lie to me.	—	—	—	—	—
8. I feel bad when I tell a lie.	—	—	—	—	—
9. It hurts my feelings when I find out someone has lied to me.	—	—	—	—	—
10. If I know someone is lying, I should point it out to them.	—	—	—	—	—
11. Lying is acceptable if no one is really hurt .	—	—	—	—	—
12. Lying is acceptable to avoid punishment.	—	—	—	—	—
13. Lying is acceptable if more good than harm comes from it.	—	—	—	—	—
14. Lying is acceptable to avoid hurting someone's feelings.	—	—	—	—	—
15. Lying is acceptable to save someone's life.	—	—	—	—	—
16. Lying is acceptable if no one will ever find out about it.	—	—	—	—	—
17. Lying is acceptable if I get what I want.	—	—	—	—	—
18. Lying is acceptable if it helps you get a job.	—	—	—	—	—
19. Lying is more acceptable if you don't really like the person.	—	—	—	—	—

<u>Using the Lying Inventory in Class</u>

After students have turned in the inventories, consider the following:

Items 1-3 deal with value judgments about lying. Report the averages of the answers to these items to the class. If there are any significant differences between the average scores on these items, how can they be explained?

Items 4-6 deal with factual judgments about lying. Ask students what the implications of any significant differences between the answers to these items and items 1-3. This might also be a good time to point out differences on individual inventories. For example, if a person strongly believes that lying is natural, are they also more inclined to disagree with the statement that lying is never acceptable? Item 5 provides an opportunity to talk about the verbal and nonverbal characteristics of liars and lying.

Items 7-9 deal with personal reactions to lying. Are there any contradictions between how a person feels when they lie versus how they feel when they are lied to? Are there any contradictions between these feelings and their value judgments about lying?

Item 10 deals with personal implications for the detection of lying. Are there any noticeable contradictions between the answer to this item and the value or personal reactions to lying?

Items 11-19 deal with the circumstances under which lying is considered acceptable. It might be informative to rank order these items according to their relative scores across the class. Under which circumstances do students think it's most acceptable to lie? Least acceptable?

After discussing these items, the instructor may also wish to discuss the following questions:
1. Will your responses to the inventory affect your interpersonal communication? How?
2. Are women or men more likely to lie in order to keep a relationship going? Why?
3. Which topics are men more likely to lie about then women?

Exercise 2: Exploring Lying on the World Wide Web

The following web exercises can be used as outside assignments or opportunities for extra credit.

1.   Read the article, "A Brief Consideration of the Ethics of Lying" by Ted Slater on the World Wide Web. The article can be located at:

   http://www.regent.edu/~tedslat/papers/lying.html

After reading this article, answer the following questions:

Do you believe lying is always wrong or that it depends on the situation? Why?

If you believe that lying is always wrong, consider the implications of this classic scenario: You live in the time of Hitler's Germany and soldiers come to the door to ask if you are hiding anyone. You are. What would you do?

If you believe that whether lying is wrong depends on the circumstances, then under which circumstances do you think it's acceptable?

Read one or more of the references at the end of the article. What is your reaction?

2.   Read the article, "Lying is part of everyday life, research confirms," found at:

   http://www.nando.net/newsroom/ntn/health/061096/health2_4146.html

After reading the article, answer the following questions:

How would you explain why women tell different kinds of lies than men do?

What does the depersonalization of society have to do with the increased incidence of lying?

Do you agree with the last paragraph of the article, that "...it would be a disaster if everyone tried to tell the truth all the time"? Why or why not?

3.   Go to the following site and read several of the posts about lying:

   http://ksi.cpsc.ucalgary.ca/PCP/1996Q/index.html#177

Report what you read to the class or conduct a class discussion about one or more of the issues at this web site.

4.   Look up "lying" on any search engine available to you and look at other sites about lying. Discuss anything you find interesting with the rest of the class.

Additional Resources

The plot of the movie, "Liar Liar" (1997) is that the lawyer-father, played by Jim Carrey, cannot lie for one full day. This results in awkward social interactions and courtroom behavior. How would your day be different if every comment from you was 100% truthful?

The entire issue of *Social Research*, Fall 1996 (v.63, n3) is devoted to articles about lying. This issue provides several outstanding articles about lying and interpersonal communication.

Other References on Lying

DePaulo, Bella M., Susan E. Kirkendol, Deborah A. Kashy, Melissa M. Wyer, and Jennifer A. Epstein. (1996). Lying In Everyday Life. *Journal of Personality and Social Psychology* 70 (May):979-997.

Ekman, Paul. (1985). *Telling Lies: Clues to Deceit in the Marketplace, Politics, and Marriage*. New York: W. W. Norton.

Fletcher, Joseph F. (1966). *Situation Ethics; The New Morality*. Philadelphia: Westminster.

Hample, Dale. (1980). Purposes and Effects of Lying. *Southern Speech Communication Journal* 46 (Fall):33-47.

Johannesen, Richard L. (1990). *Ethics in Human Communication*, 2d ed. Prospect Heights, IL: Waveland Press.

Lantos, John D. (1996). Should We Always Tell Children the Truth? *Perspectives in Biology and Medicine* 40 (Autumn):78-93.

Leslie, Larry Z. (1992). Lying in Prime Time: Ethical Egoism in Situation Comedies. *Journal of Mass Media Ethics* 7 (Spring):5-18.

Lewis, Michael. (1995). The Lying Game. *The New York Times Magazine*, April 23:24.

Lippard, Paula V. (1988). Ask Me No Questions, I'll Tell You No Lies: Situational Exigencies for Interpersonal Deception. *Western Journal of Speech Communication* 52 (Winter):119-138.

Rickman, H.P. (1995). In Praise of Lying. *Contemporary Review* 267 (Dec.):300-305.

Raised By Wolves

SELF-DISCLOSURE

"RAISED BY WOLVES"

Two distressed writers. They are experiencing complete writing block. STEVE sits with a notebook computer in his lap. KRISTEN lies down, looking at the ceiling. He vigorously types without thinking.

STEVE

Listen to me. I'm self-disclosing. I said listen, bitch.

KRISTEN

We can't say that. Besides that's an awful thing to say. Why must you constantly demean every female character you write?

STEVE

I'm just joking. I don't know what to write. Why don't you conceive the brilliant script?

KRISTEN

I'm distracted. You shouldn't have brought this vodka.

STEVE

We always drink when we write. So, don't even blame your lack of creativity on the vodka. Besides, I know why you're distracted.

KRISTEN

And why did you bring club soda? You don't drink vodka with club soda. You drink vodka with tonic. People always confuse the two. How can you confuse soda and tonic?

STEVE

I was raised by wolves, obviously.

KRISTEN

Cute.

STEVE

Are you referring to my charming wit or incredible physique?

KRISTEN

Neither. The festival deadline is tomorrow! WE MUST WRITE!

STEVE

Go ahead.

KRISTEN

I can't. I'm not the funny one. You're the funny one -- this is supposed to be funny.

George: Fine, then you write it.

Pam: No, I'm blocked.

George: Because you can't stop thinking about Phillip, the sexy transfer-student-Quentin-Tarantino-clone from Ohio who you're in lust with.

KRISTEN

That is so not true. Why would you even say something like that?

STEVE

Pam: That is not true, I'm in denial because I am fragile and scared.

George: He's just like me, you know. I thought you had a rule against falling for men who lead Maoist revolutions at video stores.

KRISTEN

Stop it, Steve.

STEVE

Pam: I have a rule against falling for anyone.

George: You want him.

KRISTEN

Pam: I do not want Phillip. He is the furthest thing from my sexual mind. And despite the empirical example of your screwed up experiences with women, platonic relationships are actually plausible. They can even be fulfilling.

STEVE

George: Do you actually expect me to believe that? Do you actually think that I don't know you well to know when you're on the verge of infatuation?

KRISTEN

Pam: That is so like you, assuming that you're omniscient.

STEVE

George: I was raised by wolves.

KRISTEN

Pam: Do you honestly think you know me well enough to just automatically override my interpretation of my emotion?

STEVE

George: I know you well enough to be able to tell when you have a crush on someone who's me except more attractive.

KRISTEN

Pam: Well maybe if you'd open your eyes and see me pining for you as you tell about every beautiful girl you take to the opera, I wouldn't be having crushes on people like Phillip --

KRISTEN (con't)
WHICH I DON'T -- but if I did, maybe -- just maybe – it's because the guy I've been completely in love with for two years took me to see <u>Independence Day</u> as an expression of my value in his life a week before he took Angela to <u>Don Giovanni</u> at the Opera House.

STEVE

George: Maybe -- just maybe -- if you weren't so cynical and took me seriously when I flirt with you constantly. Maybe . . .

KRISTEN

Don't say it.

STEVE

What?

KRISTEN

You know what.

STEVE

I hate it when you do this.

KRISTEN

What?

STEVE

What don't you want me to say, Kristen?

KRISTEN

Look, you are my very best friend in the whole wide world and I just don't want you to pretend that there's this connection between us that doesn't exist. Whenever you get bored, you allude to the possibility of ... and ... I don't know . . .

STEVE

I like you a lot. I really do.

KRISTEN

Then why has it never happened?

STEVE

Because I care about you too much to let it happen.

KRISTEN

That is such crap! Do you really think I'm so fragile and gullible as to believe that line? I didn't even believe it when I was sixteen!

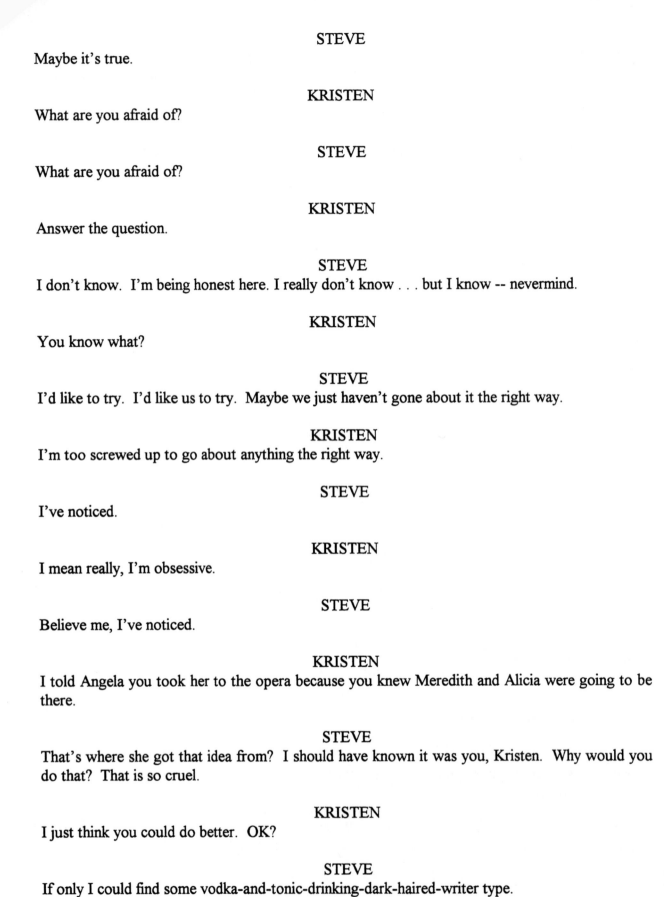

STEVE

Maybe it's true.

KRISTEN

What are you afraid of?

STEVE

What are you afraid of?

KRISTEN

Answer the question.

STEVE

I don't know. I'm being honest here. I really don't know . . . but I know -- nevermind.

KRISTEN

You know what?

STEVE

I'd like to try. I'd like us to try. Maybe we just haven't gone about it the right way.

KRISTEN

I'm too screwed up to go about anything the right way.

STEVE

I've noticed.

KRISTEN

I mean really, I'm obsessive.

STEVE

Believe me, I've noticed.

KRISTEN

I told Angela you took her to the opera because you knew Meredith and Alicia were going to be there.

STEVE

That's where she got that idea from? I should have known it was you, Kristen. Why would you do that? That is so cruel.

KRISTEN

I just think you could do better. OK?

STEVE

If only I could find some vodka-and-tonic-drinking-dark-haired-writer type.

KRISTEN

I'm right here.

STEVE

So, maybe?

KRISTEN

Maybe you should be careful what you imply.

STEVE

Why?

KRISTEN

I just might fall . . . for someone.

STEVE

And post modern girl wouldn't want that.

KRISTEN

I just want you to know what you're getting yourself into.

STEVE

You're obsessive.

KRISTEN

You're narcissistic.

STEVE

You're cynical.

KRISTEN

You're obscenely romantic.

STEVE

Otello opens next Friday.

KRISTEN

Did Angela dump you?

STEVE

Yeah.

KRISTEN

And I'm tired of being your safety net.

STEVE

I'm tired of needing one.

                                      KRISTEN
I think we wrote our script.

                                      STEVE
Naa -- not enough jokes.

                                      KRISTEN
Must everything be a comedy to you?

                                      STEVE
I was raised by wolves.

                                      KRISTEN
I don't believe you.

                                      STEVE
So -- you, me -- Otello ?

                                      KRISTEN
I can't believe you actually thought I was interested in Phillip.

                                      STEVE
I'll buy you a vodka and tonic before the show.

                                      KRISTEN
Before the opera.

                                      STEVE
Deal.

                                      KRISTEN
Date?

                                      STEVE
Date.

                              -END OF SCENE-

"RAISED BY WOLVES"—SELF-DISCLOSURE

Related Concepts in *THE INTERPERSONAL COMMUNICATION BOOK*

Primary Concepts: Unit 4: The Self in Interpersonal Communication

Self-Awareness
Self-Esteem
Self-Disclosure

Other Concepts: **Unit 2: Axioms of Interpersonal Communication**
                         Unit 15: Universals of Interpersonal Relationships
                         Unit 16: Relationship Development and Involvement
                         Unit 21: Friends and Lovers

Interpersonal Communication is a Series of Punctuated Events
Interpersonal Communications Have Content and Relationship Dimensions
Stages in Interpersonal Relationships
Relationship Development and Involvement
Friends
Lovers

Questions About "Raised by Wolves"

1. Draw a Johari Window for both Steve and Kristen before and after the discussion they have. Explain the relative sizes of the "panes" of the windows.

2. Identify a self-disclosure by Steve and by Kristen and illustrate how each meets the definition of self-disclosure as:
   - a developing process
   - a message that involves information about the self communicated to others freely or that is normally kept hidden
   - a communication to at least one other individual

3. How did the self-disclosures you identified in the question above result in further self-disclosures, which DeVito calls "the dyadic effect"?

4. Do you think there were any inappropriate self-disclosures? If so, describe them.

5. How did the circumstances of a home setting and working together affect the self-disclosures of Steve and Kristen? Make a list of the self-disclosures you can identify from the scene. Were they mostly positive or negative?

6. What rewards for the self-disclosures were evident?

7. What risks did Steve or Kristen take in self-disclosing?

8. Describe any differences in the way Steve or Kristen disclose information to one another that can be attributed to their respective genders. What gender differences in self-disclosing behavior would you generally expect in interpersonal communications?

Exercise 1: Analyzing Self-Disclosures

Analyze one self-disclosure by Steve and one by Kristen according to DeVito's guidelines:

- motivation
- appropriateness
- disclosures of the other
- burdens of the self disclosure
- gender similarities and differences

Exercise 2: "The Breakfast Club"

Watch the movie, "*The Breakfast Club*," and hold a class discussion after each student has completed the following:

Draw a Johari Window for one of the characters of the movie. Justify the size of each of the panes in the window. Do you consider this character to be self-aware? Why or why not?

Analyze the self-concept of this character according to DeVito. Specifically address the way the character's image is developed from (1) the image that others have that are revealed to them, (2) the comparisons made between theirself and others, and (3) the way they appear to interpret and evaluate their own thoughts and behaviors.

Was this character a high or low self-discloser? Were this character's self-disclosures affected by the disclosures of others? What did this character gain from self-disclosing? Did this person take unnecessary or harmful risks by self-disclosing?

Additional Resources

Relationship Issues in "Raised by Wolves"

An important aspect of this script is the relationship development issues between Steve and Kristen. Students should be able to identify some key components of relationship development. The following questions should stimulate this discussion:

What stage is the relationship in at the beginning of the clip? Which stage(s) do they go through during the clip?

Which functions does the relationship serve?

Which of the following involvement strategies are used by either Steve or Kristen (give examples)?
•directness
•endurance
•indirect suggestion
•public presentation
•separation
•third party
•triangle

Which nonverbal behaviors illustrate the direction that this relationship is taking?

Other References on Self-Disclosure

Berger, Stephen E., Millham, Jim, Jacobson, Leonard I., and Anchor, Kenneth N. (1978). Prior Self Disclosure, Sex Differences, and Actual Confiding in an Interpersonal Encounter. *Small Group Behavior* 9 (Nov.):555-562.

Derlega, Valerian J. (1993). *Self-Disclosure*. Newbury Park, Calif.: Sage.

Derlega, Valerian J. and Alan L. Chaikin. (1975). *Sharing Intimacy: What We Reveal to Others and Why*. Englewood Cliffs, N.J.: Prentice-Hall.

Dindia, Kathryn. (1982). Reciprocity of Self-Disclosure: A Sequential Analysis. *Communication Yearbook* 6:506-528.

Hugenberg, Lawrence W., Sr., and Mark J. Schaefermeyer. (1983). Soliloquy as Self Disclosure. *Quarterly Journal of Speech* 69 (May):180-187.

McCroskey, James C. and Virginia P. Richmond. (1977). Communication Apprehension as a Predictor of Self-Disclosure. *Communication Quarterly* 25 (Fall):40-43.

Powell, John J. (1969). *Why Am I Afraid to Tell You Who I Am?* Chicago: Argus Communications.

Rosenfeld, Lawrence R. (1979). Self-Disclosure Avoidance: Why I Am Afraid To Tell You Who I Am. *Communication Monographs* 46 (March):63-74.

Wheeless, Lawrence R. (1976). Self-Disclosure and Interpersonal Solidarity: Measurement, Validation, and Relationships. *Human Communication Research* 3 (Fall):47-61.

Wheeless, Lawrence R., and Janis Grotz. (1977). The Measurement of Trust and Its Relationship to Self-Disclosure. *Human Communication Research* 3 (Spring):250-257.

Wheeless, Lawrence R., Kathryn Nesser, and James C. McCroskey. (1986). The Relationships of Self-Disclosure and Disclosiveness to High and Low Communication Apprehension. *Communication Research Reports* 3 (Dec.):129-134.

Check, Please

APPREHENSION AND ASSERTIVENESS

"CHECK, PLEASE"

SHENITA sits at a restaurant table with an empty cup of coffee. A pile of books and papers sits by her side. An overwhelmed waitress passes by.

SHENITA

Excuse me.

WAITRESS

Just a second, okay? What can I get for you?

SHENITA

I've been waiting for a cup of coffee for about twenty minutes now.

WAITRESS

I'm really sorry.

SHENITA

Is it that difficult to pour a cup of coffee?

WAITRESS

Well, we're kinda busy. This is only my second day.

SHENITA

Just bring me some coffee.

WAITRESS

Consider it done. Anything else?

SHENITA

I said -- just coffee.

WAITRESS

No problem.

SHENITA

Thushari! Over here.

THUSHARI

I'm so sorry I'm late. I had to pick up my cat from the vet and they were running behind. Oh, did she leave already? I'm really sorry.

SHENITA

You're . . . It's no big deal. Victoria isn't even here yet.

THUSHARI

Oh, good. Not that she isn't here but that . . .

SHENITA

I understand. You know, it's impossible to get a cup of coffee here. Waitress!

WAITRESS

There you go.

THUSHARI

Could I get a menu?

SHENITA

I can't believe that. Does she not understand the concept of being tipped?

THUSHARI

It's packed in here.

SHENITA

I don't care. This is her job. She should be able to handle a full restaurant. Did you want to order something?

THUSHARI

It's no big deal.

SHENITA

Sure it is. Waitress!

THUSHARI

Really, it's OK.

SHENITA

Well, you were going to order before and she left, right?

THUSHARI

Yeah, but I don't . . .

SHENITA

Excuse me! Coffee girl!!

THUSHARI

Shenita, don't.

WAITRESS

What can I do for you?

SHENITA

She wanted to order something!

THUSHARI

I don't want to order anything now. I changed my mind.

WAITRESS

Okay. Was everything else okay?

SHENITA

I could use some more coffee. Preferably warm!

WAITRESS

Sure. Was it cold before?

SHENITA

It wasn't warm.

WAITRESS

I'm really sorry. Everything's going wrong today. I'll get you a fresh cup of coffee. I've got to go.

SHENITA

This class is so difficult. There is way too much reading.

THUSHARI

Yeah.

SHENITA

It's like she doesn't even realize that we have four other classes and jobs and heaven forbid -- lives.

THUSHARI

It is hard.

SHENITA

And she is so incredible. I mean, she's so harsh and alienating. I'm afraid to go to her classes sometimes.

WAITRESS

(*brings another cup of coffee*) It's on the house.

THUSHARI

She's different.

SHENITA

If I didn't have to take this class to graduate in the spring, I'd be gone. Everyone left in her class says the same thing.

THUSHARI

I don't have to take it.

SHENITA

You're a history major, right?

THUSHARI

Yeah. But I don't have to take it. I'm retaking it.

SHENITA

Why?

THUSHARI

I wasn't happy with my grade.

SHENITA

What was it?

THUSHARI

A "B".

SHENITA

You're retaking this class with this woman because of a "B"? That's insane.

THUSHARI

Yeah, I guess it's crazy. Maybe I'll drop it.

SHENITA

I would.

THUSHARI

Maybe I will.

SHENITA

After our presentation, though.

THUSHARI

What time is it?

SHENITA

11:30. She's half an hour late.

50

THUSHARI

I have an eight o'clock class in the morning.

SHENITA

Well, do you have any ideas about the presentation?

THUSHARI

No. Do you?

SHENITA

I guess not. I just don't want do a boring generic presentation, like, "I'll take 550 through 450 BC, and you take 450 to 350 BC and we will all talk for five minutes. I mean, I hate presentations like that.

THUSHARI

I do too.

SHENITA

It's always obvious that people didn't put much time into it when they do it like that. And it's like what's the point of a group presentation.

THUSHARI

I agree.

SHENITA

There's Victoria.

VICTORIA

The most ridiculous thing just happened to me. I can't even believe it. Does anyone work here?

SHENITA

You have to flag her down.

VICTORIA

So, I'm at the grocery store, right, and this guy starts screaming things like, "Monkey, Monkey, Monkey." Then, he starts pointing at stuff in the store and screaming out product names. Like, he would point at the juice display and scream, "Sunny Delight!" or "Fudge Frosted Pop Tarts." I'm completely serious!

THUSHARI

I'm sure you are. But we need to get started. It's late.

VICTORIA

I was just telling a story. It's almost over.

THUSHARI

You were half an hour late to begin with. We need to get started. We don't have much time.

VICTORIA

We don't need that much time. I was thinking we'd just divide up the material. Like, you could do 550-450 BC. I could do 450-350. Then we could set a time limit for each section. That way we can work whenever its best with our schedules. Right, Shenita?

SHENITA

That's fine, I guess. If that's what the two of you want to do.

VICTORIA

Great, so, how should we divide this?

THUSHARI

Now, wait a second. Shenita and I think that we should do something more creative. Each of us speaking for five minutes is not going to cut it in this class. What do you think, Shenita?

SHENITA

Well. I wouldn't mind putting a little more work into this.

VICTORIA

Look. I have a lot of stuff to do this week. I have two mid-terms and I work forty hours a week.

THUSHARI

So do I. But this is a group project. We need to work as a group.

VICTORIA

I understand that but let's be realistic. I can't afford to put that much time into this. We'll be fine if we do it my way. I bet 90% of the class will organize their presentations like that.

THUSHARI

Why shouldn't we be in the top ten percent?

VICTORIA

Because that's not a priority.

THUSHARI

Well, maybe not to you. But I think that we should put a little more work into it and be a little more creative. Well, it's up to Shenita now. Shenita?

VICTORIA

Shenita wants . . .

THUSHARI

I was asking Shenita.

SHENITA

Look, I'm very busy. But, I think you're right, Thushari. We should really try to do a nice presentation. I mean, I have an early class in the morning, but if you guys want to stay late I can do that.

THUSHARI

Okay. Shenita had some really great ideas.

SHENITA

Okay. I was thinking that maybe we could . . .

VICTORIA

Where is that waitress? I think I need a cup of coffee.

-END OF SCENE-

"CHECK, PLEASE!"—APPREHENSION AND ASSERTIVENESS

Related Concepts in *THE INTERPERSONAL COMMUNICATION BOOK*

Primary Concepts: Unit 5: Apprehension and Assertiveness

Speaker Apprehension
       The Nature of Speaker Apprehension
       Theories of Speaker Apprehension and Its Management
       Empowering Apprehensives
Assertiveness

Other Concepts: **Unit 3: Culture in Interpersonal Communication**
                      Unit 4: The Self in Interpersonal Communication
                      Unit 8: Effectiveness in Interpersonal Communication
                      Unit 9: Universals of Verbal and Nonverbal Messages
                      Unit 10: Verbal Messages: Principles and Pitfalls
                      Unit 12: Nonverbal Messages: Body and Sound
                      Unit 19: Power in Interpersonal Relationships

Culture in Interpersonal Communication
       How Cultures Differ
Self-Concept
A Pragmatic Model of Interpersonal Effectiveness
Meanings and Messages
       Meanings are More Than Words and Gestures
       Meanings are Context-Based
Message Characteristics
       Messages Are Packaged
Disconfirmation and Confirmation
Facial Communication
Eye Communication
Power in Interpersonal Relationships

Questions about "Check, Please"

1. How is Shenita's behavior different (verbally and nonverbally) when communicating with:

   The waitress

   Thushari

   Victoria

2. How would you explain these differences?

3. How is Thusari's behavior (verbally and nonverbally) different in communicating with:

   Shenita

   the waitress.

   Victoria

4. How would you explain these differences?

Exercise 1: An Assertiveness Diary

1. Make a list of situations in the past where you found yourself being less assertive than you would have liked to be.

2. Next, keep a diary for one week of situations where you were less assertive than you would have liked to be.

3. At the end of the week, compare your original list with you diary and compile one list that includes all of the items from both lists.

4. At the end of your combined list, describe how you feel you should have responded to the situations on this list.

5. Keep a diary for one more week, and note any improvements you feel you have made in your assertiveness behavior.

6. Repeat steps 4 and 5 until you are satisfied with your assertiveness behavior.

Exercise #2: Practicing Assertive Behavior

1. Choose three situations where you find yourself not being as assertive, or being more aggressive, than you would prefer being.
2. For each situation, write down what you believe are the reasons for your nonassertivess or aggressiveness.
3. Next, write down how you would prefer to behave in those circumstances.
4. Role play your preferred behavior with another person.
5. Finally, answer the following questions:

> Did you feel better behaving more assertively/less aggressively?
> Was it more or less difficult than you thought it would be?
> Are there other preferable behavioral choices than the ones you identified?
> Do you think you will be able to put these behavioral changes into effect?

Additional Resources

The November 1995 edition of *Psychology Today* (Vol. 28, No. 6), under the cover article, "Are You Shy?" contains an excellent set of articles about shyness, including titles such as:

The Natural History of Shyness
Helping Others Beat Shyness
We Shall Overcome
The Shy Brain
1995 *Psychology Today* Survey on Shyness (a survey students could take in class)
Helping Shy Kids

Columnist Laura Lippman wrote a series of articles about shyness, especially as it relates to the profoundly shy behavior of several famous celebrities such as Carol Burnett, Johnny Carson, David Letterman, Barbra Streisand, and others. The articles do a respectable job of addressing the issues of shyness as inherited or learned. The articles can be found in:

The Baltimore Sun (Shy Away: Unabashedly Bashful: Researchers are Discovering That Some People Are Shy From Birth While Others Just Feel Shy in Certain Circumstances, February 27, 1996, FINAL EDITION, Pg. 1E) .

The Dallas Morning News (Mending Our Shy Ways: Celebrities Are Not Alone In Dealing With Bashfulness, March 6, 1996, Pg. 1C).

St. Louis Post-Dispatch (The Silent [Almost] Majority Who Are Shy: Almost Half of Americans Asked Say They Suffer From It, March 25, 1996, Pg. 4E).

Other Sources on Apprehension and Assertiveness

Breidenstein-Cutspec, Patricia, and Elizabeth Goering. (1989). Exploring Cultural Diversity: A Network Analysis of the Communicative Correlates of Shyness Within the Black Culture. *Communication Research Reports* 6 (June):37-46.

Brody, Jane E. (1989). The Effects of Shyness Can Cripple; But Therapists Help In Hurdling Barriers. *The San Diego Union Tribune* (Nov. 20):C1

Cutspec, Patricia, and Elizabeth Goering. (1988). Acknowledging Cultural Diversity: Perceptions of Shyness Within the Black Culture. *Howard Journal of Communications* 1 (Spring):75-87.

Duran, Robert L., and Lynne Kelly. (1989). The Cycle of Shyness: A Study of Self-Perceptions of Communication Performance. *Communication Reports* 2 (Winter):30-38.

Goering, Elizabeth, and Patricia Breidenstein-Cutspec. (1989). The Web of Shyness: A Network Analysis of Communicative Correlates. *Communication Research Reports* 6 (Dec.):111-118.

Goering, Elizabeth M. and Patricia Breidenstein-Cutspec. (1990). The Co-Cultural Experience of Shyness: A Comparison of the Friendship Networks of Black Communicators and White Communicators. *Howard Journal of Communications* 2 (Summer):262-275.

Kelly, Lynne. (1982). A Rose By Any other Name Is Still A Rose: A Comparative Analysis of Reticence, Communication Apprehension, Unwillingness to Communicate, and Shyness. *Human Communication Research* 8 (Winter):99-113.

McCroskey, James C., and Virginia P. Richmond. (1982). Communication Apprehension and Shyness: Conceptual and Operational Distinctions. *Central States Speech Journal* 33 (Fall):458-468.

Prisbell, Marshall. (1985). Assertiveness, Shyness, and Nonverbal Communicative Behaviors. *Communication Research Reports* 2 (Dec.):120-127.

Prisbell, Marshall. (1986). The Relationship Between Assertiveness and Dating Behavior Among College Students. *Communication Research Reports* 3 (Dec.):9-12.

Prisbell, Marshall. (1988). Perception Difference and Levels of Shyness. *Communication Research Reports* 5 (Dec.):197-203.

Prisbell, Marshall. (1991). Shyness and Self-Reported Competence. *Communication Research Reports* 8 (Dec.):141-148.

Singhal, Arvind, and Mokoto Nagao. (1993). Assertiveness As Communication Competence: A Comparison of the Communication Styles of American and Japanese Students. *Asian Journal of Communication* 3:1-18.

Zakahi, Walter R. (1985). The Relationship of Assertiveness to Communicative Competence and Communication Satisfaction: A Dyadic Assessment. *Communication Research Reports* 2 (Dec.):36-40.

PSA #136

VERBAL PITFALLS

"PSA #136"

A small party. ELIZABETH, LIBBY, and JONATHAN are standing in a small circle. Music is playing softly in the background. Elizabeth is overcompensating for the background noise, talking a bit too loudly.

VOICE-OVER
It's the hottest party of the year. That special someone is talking to you. Then out of the blue, you are struck by a verbal pitfall. I think I hear one now. . . .

ELIZABETH
So - we're debating Michigan, right. . . . Michigan. It's 4-3. It's break round. And the stakes are really high. I mean we've had a bad year, and we're not doing well on the Aff. HDR - Hot Dry Rocks. Sullivan is prepping them before the round.

JONATHAN
Sullivan?

ELIZABETH
The D.O.F.

JONATHAN
Director of . . . ?

ELIZABETH
Forensics. Director of Forensics. So anyway, Sullivan is prepping them, but the pressure is intense. We haven't been under this much pressure since the NDT. The 1NC gets up and reads the normal offcase stuff -- Clinton, Business confidence, Saudi oil, Require T - then this funky counterplan, ISO14000 and I completely zone out -- I mean I ask Jack to write some answers and he freaks out -- he can't remember a single thing. I'm like "Jack just write some perms -- some link take-outs, you know -- no threshold, no internal link, just some, some unique arguments," and he completely refuses.

JONATHAN
Listen, this conversation is enthralling and all but I -- I need to check on the dry ice. I'll be back.

LIBBY
See you - *Jonathan exits* - later. Liz, you're doing it again.

ELIZABETH
What?

LIBBY
You're completely ruining my chances with Jonathan.

ELIZABETH

I refuse to listen to this again. You know just because you can't hold your crush of the month interest, don't blame me.

LIBBY

Because you bore them.

ELIZABETH

Well excuse me if I interrupted your monologue about crop circles.

LIBBY

Aliens are very trendy -- and we were talking about last Friday's episode of "The X-Files." Jonathan loves "The X-Files". . . . but he can never love me.

ELIZABETH

Just try a little harder. Undo some buttons, talk about botany -- I don't know. Look, he's coming this way. He's coming back -- don't panic.

JONATHAN

Why aren't you two dancing?

Neither respond. Elizabeth looks at Libby as if to say "you better say something or he's going to think you're a dork."

LIBBY

I'm not much for dancing. *Elizabeth nudges her.* I've had a little bit too much to drink. *Elizabeth nudges her again* -- But I hear you're a great dancer.

JONATHAN

You know, I always wanted to be a dancer. I took tap dancing lessons when I was a kid.

LIBBY

Really?

JONATHAN

I was in a dance recital once. Really. Guess what I was.

LIBBY

I have no idea.

JONATHAN

Come on, guess.

ELIZABETH

Oh, can I guess? A tap-dancing fire engine?

LIBBY

A sunflower?

JONATHAN

The boys didn't play the flowers. I was the wise oak tree. But Cynthia Wagner, my next door neighbor who was also my first kiss, she was a sunflower.

ELIZABETH

You don't say.

JONATHAN

It's true.

LIBBY

Sexy -- sensitive -- and intelligent.

JONATHAN

What?

ELIZABETH

Libby was just saying what a great party this is.

JONATHAN

Isn't it? You know what the secret to throwing a great party is? More men. Lots of different types of people. If most of the people at the party only know one or two other people at the party, then they are forced to mingle with people they don't know. I once had this Christmas party where I invited five random people from each of my classes. I didn't even know them. I was kind of nervous, but it turned out great. You see everyone was real shy, but then they all realized that they had to talk to someone they didn't know. Three relationships started that night. And they're all still together. Some people just throw great parties. Really.

There is a pause for a few beats.

ELIZABETH

Well, this is one great party.

LIBBY

Definitely.

ELIZABETH

Hey, do you remember that party at USC --that New Year's eve party -- last year? Jack went out of control and "broken arm boy" chipped his tooth. He was such an idiot -- and Seamus . . .

LIBBY

Do you want to dance?

JONATHAN

I thought you'd never ask. *They begin to walk away and dance.* You know lots of girls have a hard time asking men to dance. I remember when I was in high school, my sister Rachel -- do you know her? Anyway, Rachel . . . *Their conversation fades away.*

Elizabeth is left standing alone. She looks around for a place to sit, doesn't see anyplace. She looks around, looking awkward.

-END OF SCENE-

"PSA #136" - VERBAL PITFALLS

Related Concepts in *THE INTERPERSONAL COMMUNICATION BOOK*

Primary Concepts: Unit 10: Verbal Messages: Principles and Pitfalls

Talking up, talking down, and talking equal
Confirmation and disconfirmation
Racism, sexism, heterosexism
Inclusion and exclusion
Balance of self-talk and other-talk
Criticism, honest appraisal and praise

Other Concepts:

    Unit 2: Axioms of Interpersonal Communication
    Unit 3: Culture in Interpersonal Communication
    Unit 4: The Self in Interpersonal Communication
    Unit 5: Apprehension and Assertiveness
    Unit 6: Perception in Interpersonal Communication
    Unit 7: Listening in Interpersonal Communication
    Unit 8: Effectiveness in Interpersonal Communication
    Unit 9: Universals of Verbal and Nonverbal Messages

Interpersonal Communication is a Transactional Process
Communication is Inevitable, Irreversible and Unrepeatable
Interpersonal Communication is a Process of Adjustment
Interpersonal Communications Have Content and Relationship Dimensions
High- and Low-Context Cultures
Uncertainty Reduction
Social Comparisons
Self-Esteem
Self-Disclosure
Speaker Apprehension
Increasing Accuracy in Interpersonal Perceptions
Effective Listening
Mindfulness
Immediacy
Interaction Management
Other-Orientation
Meanings Are in People

Questions About "PSA #136"

Let's consider each of the persons in this party scene -- Elizabeth, Libby, and Jonathan--and ways that their conversations might alienate others.

1. What examples of "talking down" and "talking up" did you notice between Elizabeth and Libby? between Libby and Jonathan? when Jonathan talks to both Elizabeth and Libby?

2. What examples of disconfirmation and exclusion did you notice in conversations between Elizabeth and Libby? between Libby and Jonathan? when Jonathan talks to both Elizabeth and Libby?

3. How would you describe the self-talk and other-talk by Elizabeth? Libby? Jonathan? How do you perceive persons who talk down to you (condescending, patronizing)? What are some ways of responding to such situations?

4. How would you re-write these conversations to be more confirming, balanced, and other-oriented?

5. Based on these party conversations, what outcomes would you predict for the relationship between Elizabeth and Libby? between Elizabeth and Jonathan? between Libby and Jonathan?

Exercise 1: Are You Bristling?*

Bristles are behaviors or statements by another person to which you respond in a sensitized and negative way, i.e., you bristle. When you are on the receiving end of verbal pitfalls, you may find yourself "bristling." Bristles are often identified when a person says, "It really bugs me when . . . ." Often, as a result of such statements and actions, you perceive the other person to be inconsiderate, insincere, uninformed, etc.

Write down the verbal pitfalls or behaviors made by others (friends, family, teachers, supervisors, etc.) that bristle you.

What might you do or say that bristles others -- friends, family, teachers, supervisors, etc.)?

What might you do to adjust your own bristle statements and behaviors?

Follow-Up Questions

Ask students to explain how others' comments and behaviors bristle them.

How do you react and respond to verbal pitfalls/bristles?

How might your own comments and behaviors bristle others? When you notice that others are reacting and bristling to a comment you have made, what might you do to explore those reactions and improve the situation?

*Adapted from Civikly-Powell, J. Classroom Teaching Skills, Teaching Assistant Resource Center, University of New Mexico.

Exercise 2: Observing Social Group Interactions

This exercise may serve as an outside assignment or perhaps one for extra credit. Instruct students to select a segment from a television show or a movie that depicts communication during a social gathering, e.g., a party, a dinner, a celebration, etc.

The student's analysis should include an overview of the scene (including the number and names of characters) followed by explanations of verbal pitfall behaviors observed in the scene. You may want to offer extra credit for suggestions given to improve/remedy each pitfall.

NAME OF TV SHOW OR MOVIE _____

CHARACTERS' NAMES & ROLES_____

_____

_____

_____

OVERVIEW OF THE SCENE

VERBAL PITFALL	EXAMPLE	REMEDY
Excluding Talk		
Disconfirming Talk		
Imbalance Talk		
Criticism		

Additional Resources

Clips from Woody Allen films are excellent for analysis of conversations and relationships, e.g., *Annie Hall*, *Hannah and Her Sisters*, and *Manhattan*.

Film: *"Who's Afraid of Virginia Woolf?"*

Examples from television shows (e.g., *3rd Rock From The Sun*, *Star Trek* and its progeny), "bloopers" shows, commercials, etc.

George Carlin's recording of "Seven Deadly Words."

Visit chat lines on the Internet that have specialized vocabularies, e.g., computer-savvy groups, scientific groups, gay and lesbian groups, ethnic groups.

Search "jargon" on any Web search engine for sources that discuss computer and Internet jargon.

Other References on Verbal Pitfalls

Cowan, John (1996). Lessons From the Playground. In Kathleen M. Galvin and Pamela Cooper (Eds.), *Making Connections: Readings in Relational Communication*, pp. 291-292, Los Angeles: Roxbury Publishing.

Cupach, William R. (1994). Social Predicaments. In William R. Cupach and Brian H. Spitzberg (Eds.), *The Dark Side of Interpersonal Communication*, pp. 159-180, Hillsdale, New Jersey: Lawrence Erlbaum.

Fisher, Roger & Scott Brown (1988). *Getting Together: Building a Relationship that Gets to Yes*. Boston: Houghton Mifflin.

Gilligan, Carol (1982). *In a Different Voice*. Cambridge, Massachusetts: Harvard University Press.

Ivy, Diana K. and Phil Backlund (1994). *Exploring Genderspeak*. New York: McGraw Hill.

Nash, Waler (1993). *Jargon: Its Uses and Abuses*. Cambridge, MA: Oxford.

Tannen, Deborah (1990). *You Just Don't Understand*. New York: William Morrow.

Watzlawick, Paul, Janet B. Bavelas and Don D. Jackson (1967). *Pragmatics of Human Communication*. New York: W.W. Norton.

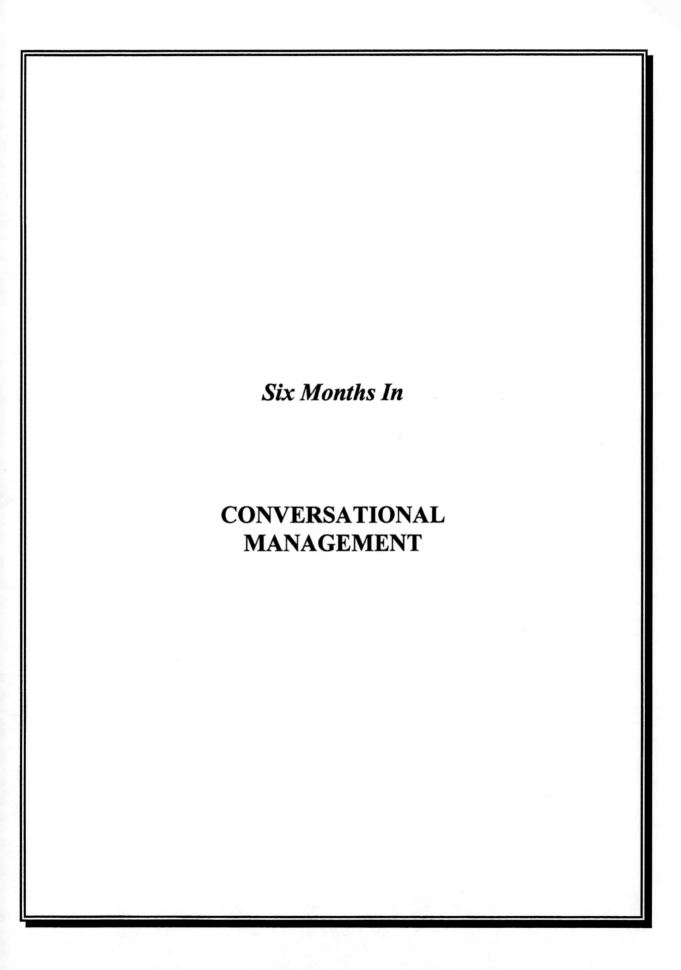

Six Months In

**CONVERSATIONAL
MANAGEMENT**

"SIX MONTHS IN"

A small kitchen. SUSANNA sits with her morning coffee. MIKE enters, hazy and sleepy eyed

MIKE

Good morning. *He kisses Susanna on the cheek and she pushes him away.*

SUSANNA

Brush your teeth.

MIKE

Is there coffee?

SUSANNA

Isn't there always?

MIKE

Now that you mention it, yes. There's always coffee when you're here. Wow. Thank you.

SUSANNA

Don't mention it.

He pours himself a cup.

MIKE

Is there cream?

SUSANNA

In the fridge.

MIKE

That makes sense. *He puts cream in his coffee.* What about the. . . (*he turns around and she is extending the sugar towards him.*) sugar? Thank you again.

SUSANNA

Don't mention it -- again.

MIKE

It's great having you here. Really. When you're not here, which isn't often, I really miss you.

SUSANNA

Do you?

MIKE

I do. You know I was thinking. . . . I was thinking how you spend so much time here -- and when you're not here, I'm at your place -- and we're both so broke and -- both paying rent, and . . .

SUSANNA

Mike, I was thinking about that too. And I was thinking . . . . we need to talk.

MIKE

Yeah, I was thinking that too.

SUSANNA

Good.

MIKE

Okay.

SUSANNA

All right. Well, I've only been home one night this week . . .

MIKE

Saturday, and I was with you. We stayed at your place that night.

SUSANNA

Yes. I was only home Saturday and you were with me. Every other night I've been here . . .

MIKE

That was after Adrianna's Halloween party! We stayed at your place because it was closer . . .

SUSANNA

Yes. And if we hadn't been closer to my apartment we probably would have been here. Now, I like your place and all . . .

MIKE

It's a nice place. It's cheap. It's close to your work. It's quiet . . .

SUSANNA

Can you please just let me finish what I'm trying to say -- this is difficult okay . . .

MIKE

More coffee?

SUSANNA

Can you please shut-up for like thirty seconds!

MIKE

Sorry. You just looked like you needed more coffee. In fact you do. I'm going to get you more coffee. I'm sorry Susan. I do this all the time, don't I? I never let you finish a thought. I'm trying to stop doing that. Really I am. I have a short attention span. I've always had a short attention span. They wanted to put me on Ritalin when I was in elementary school. My mom wouldn't let them. Susanna, I'm trying, but then you start with this scary "we need to talk," and all of the sudden I feel like just as I'm getting ready to ask you something very important you're about to break up with me and I don't want to hear it.

SUSANNA

Are you done with your monologue?

MIKE

I guess.

SUSANNA

Are you ready to let me speak?

MIKE

Yes - after I get you more coffee.

SUSANNA

I think that we should take a break from each other . . . for awhile. *She looks at him. He looks at her.*

MIKE

Do you want me to talk now?

SUSANNA

Of course I want you to talk now. I just said I think we should take some time off. Don't you have anything to say about that?

MIKE

Well, you just told me not to talk.

SUSANNA

I asked you to let me finish my thought. I finished my thought. You can talk now. You should talk now.

MIKE

No coffee?

SUSANNA

Mike!

MIKE

Okay, well . . . why?

SUSANNA

I just said. Look, we're with each other all of the time. Every waking second.

MIKE

Don't you like spending time with me?

SUSANNA

Of course I do -- but, you're confusing the question.

MIKE

If you like spending time with me, what's wrong with spending lots of time with me?

SUSANNA

Nothing's wrong with it. I just said I think we should take some time off. What do you think about that?

MIKE

What do you mean?

SUSANNA

I mean do you think it's a good idea?

Mike takes a deep breath, exhales. He looks at the floor. She looks at him. He pauses.

MIKE

Sure. If you think that's best.

SUSANNA

What do you think?

MIKE

Well, I don't want to.

SUSANNA

Mike, I love being with you. But, I need some time to myself too. If I don't have that time -- time alone, I begin to feel suffocated. And when I feel suffocated I begin to resent you for little things - like not knowing the half and half is in the refrigerator. And when I begin to resent you for not knowing the half and half is in the refrigerator, I begin to not like being with you. And when I begin to not like being with you I begin to want to break up with you. Does that make sense?

MIKE

I guess.

SUSANNA

What doesn't make sense about it?

MIKE

Look, I understand what you're saying, but you can't blame me for not agreeing. If you need some time away, that's your deal. I don't though.

SUSANNA

Fine, but you understand I need some time?

MIKE

What if we spend more time at your place?

SUSANNA

It's not about where we're at. It's about the fact that I need time to do other things and spend time with other people. You should spend time with other people too. Too much of a good thing isn't a good thing. Don't you miss going out with your friends?

MIKE

What if we just limited the amount of time we spend together? Like, decide we only will see each other three times a week?

SUSANNA

We could do that. *She takes a deep breath.*

MIKE

But . . .

SUSANNA

I would rather just make a clean break for at least a week. Is that okay with you?

MIKE

I'm just afraid that if we take some time off that you'll never want to come back.

SUSANNA

I don't think that will happen.

MIKE

But what if it does?

SUSANNA

We'd deal with it then.

MIKE

You have an answer for everything. How do you do that? When we have these talks it's about as much as I can do to listen.

SUSANNA

You're a good listener. That's one of the things I love about you. We just have to get you talking more often - well, maybe not more often - but more relevantly.

MIKE

What else do you love about me?

SUSANNA

So can we take a break?

MIKE

Yes, but I won't give you my blessing.

SUSANNA

Is this okay with you?

MIKE

Do you want me to lie?

SUSANNA

No.

MIKE

It's fine. We have been spending too much time together. The guys at work say I'm woman-owned. It's funny, because I used to joke right along with them when other guys would talk about their girlfriends, and now I see nothing wrong with it. But my woman does.

SUSANNA

I just need some time to think -- before you ask me to move in with you.

MIKE

You saw that coming, huh? *She nods her head.* What can I say? *singing* "I'm as bright and as gay as a daisy in May a cliché coming true." *She glares at him lovingly.* Relevant- I'm being relevant. . . . Take as much time as you need. Then we'll work it out when it happens. Eh? I'm learning.

SUSANNA

Quick study. But do you believe these lines you've memorized?

MIKE

Yes, I do.

SUSANNA

And next time I'm here you better have some decent coffee 'cause this is crap.

MIKE

Promise. . . . So. . .

SUSANNA

So.

                                    MIKE
I have work. You have class. I have to get in the shower.

                                  SUSANNA
Oh, yeah.

                                    MIKE
I guess this is farewell.

                                  SUSANNA
Wow! So I tell you I need a break and you end up kicking me out?

                                    MIKE
No, I'm not kicking you out. I just really need to get going. I was late yesterday. You can stick
around if you want. . . .

                                  SUSANNA
No, I should get going and get some real coffee before my Economics test.

                                    MIKE
That's today?

                                  SUSANNA
Today I face my death.

                                    MIKE
You'll ace it -- you always do.

                                  SUSANNA
Okay. Well thanks for understanding.

                                    MIKE
Don't mention it.

                                  SUSANNA
And tell the guys at work it was your idea. . . . I'll call you in a few days.

                                    MIKE
Okay.

                                  SUSANNA
You sure?

                                    MIKE
Would you get out of here, you're suffocating me.

                              SUSANNA
Bye.

                                MIKE
Until we meet again. *He kisses her hand. She leaves.*

                          -END OF SCENE-

"SIX MONTHS IN" - CONVERSATIONAL MANAGEMENT

Related Concepts in *THE INTERPERSONAL COMMUNICATION BOOK*

Primary Concepts: Unit 14: Messages and Conversation

Initiating Conversations
>   Self-, other-, relational- and context-references

Maintaining Conversations
>   Speaker Cues: turn-taking, turn-maintaining, turn-yielding
>   Listener Cues: turn-requesting, turn-denying, back channeling messages
>   Interruptions
>>   confirming and disconfirming
>>   functions
>>   gender
>   Monologue and Dialogue Communication
>   Disclaimers
>   Excuses

Closing Conversations
>   Summarizing
>   Ending
>   Expressing enjoyment
>   Referring to future

Other Concepts: **Unit 7: Listening;**
Unit 9: Universals of Verbal and Nonverbal Messages;
Unit 15: Universals of Interpersonal Relationships
Unit 17: Relationship Deterioration and Dissolution

Listening, culture and gender
Participatory and passive listening
Empathic and objective listening
Nonjudgmental and critical listening
Surface and depth listening
Active listening
Meanings are in people
Stages in interpersonal relationships
Stages of relationship deterioration
Strategies of disengagement
Some causes of relationship deterioration

1. How would you characterize the start of this conversation? Did you hear Self-, other-, relational- and/or context-references?

2. How would you describe Susanna's conversational style?

3. How would you describe Mike's conversational style?

4. What types of interruptions did you notice in this conversation? Did you notice any interruption behaviors that differed for Mike and Susanna? Does gender play a role in interruption behaviors?

5. Why might Susanna be frustrated with this conversation?

6. Why might Mike be frustrated with this conversation?

7. Are there parts of this conversation that seem to work well? If so, what is happening in these parts?

8. How would you characterize the closing of this conversation? Did you hear/see summarizing? ending? expressing enjoyment? referring to the future?

9. How would you describe Mike's listening behavior?

10. At what stage would you characterize Susanna and Mike's relationship?

11. What predictions to you have for Susanna and Mike's relationship?

Exercise 1: Good Talker? Good Listener?

Have students form dyads and provide each student with instructions about having a 5-10 minute conversation. Students should know that they are meeting a friend and the students can decide if the meeting is for lunch or for a drink later in the afternoon.

Note: A variation of this exercise is for students to work in groups of 4, with 2 students conducting their conversation which the other 2 students observe. When completed, reverse roles, so that each dyad has an opportunity to conduct their conversation and an opportunity to observe and provide feedback.

Instructions for Person A

You've made plans to meet a friend of yours for lunch (or for a drink later in the afternoon). Both of you have very busy schedules and it has taken several weeks to coordinate this time to get together. You want to tell your friend about the things that have been going on in your life (work, friends, school, relationships, projects, etc.). You are an attentive listener and a good talker. You are looking forward to having time to spend with your friend.

Instructions for Person B

You've made plans to meet a friend of yours for lunch (or for a drink later in the afternoon). Both of you have very busy schedules and it has taken several weeks to coordinate this time to get together. You want to tell your friend about the things that have been going on in your life (work, friends, school, relationships, projects, etc.). You're not too attentive during conversations and are easily distracted by things you want to say and by what is going on around you. You have a habit of interrupting before the other person finishes speaking and of allowing for longer pauses (silence) than is usually expected in a casual conversation.

Follow-up Questions

How would you describe the conversation in which you participated?

What examples did you notice of speaker cues during the conversation: turn-taking, turn-maintaining, turn-yielding?

What examples did you notice of listener cues during the conversation: turn-requesting, turn-denying, back channeling messages?

What examples did you notice of monologue communication, dialogue communication, disclaimers and excuses?

Exercise 2: Script Analysis

The interaction between Susanna and Mike is a good resource for examining conversations. Complete this chart, citing examples to depict each of the behaviors as demonstrated by Susanna and Mike.

COMMUNICATION BEHAVIOR	SUSANNA	MIKE
Initiating Conversations		
self-references	_____	_____
other-references	_____	_____
relational-references	_____	_____
context-references	_____	_____
Speaker Cues		
turn-taking	_____	_____
turn-maintaining	_____	_____
turn-yielding	_____	_____
Listener Cues		
turn-requesting	_____	_____
turn-denying	_____	_____
back channeling messages	_____	_____
Confirming Responses	_____	_____
Disconfirming Responses	_____	_____
Monologue Communication	_____	_____
Dialogue Communication	_____	_____
Disclaimers	_____	_____
Excuses	_____	_____
Closing Conversations		
summarizing	_____	_____
ending	_____	_____
expressing enjoyment	_____	_____
referring to the future	_____	_____

Additional Resources

Scripts: Most of Woody Allen's plays and screenplays are excellent resources, e.g., *Annie Hall*, Hannah and Her Sisters, and *Manhattan*.

Public conversations are interesting to compare to private conversations, as are private conversations that take place in public. Eavesdrop on some conversations and examine the concepts about conversational management.

Other ways that private conversations become public are radio and television talk shows. And, on the Internet, there are IRCs -- Internet Relay Chat groups and discussion groups where you can follow others conversations, even if you don't participate.

Other References on Conversational Management

Benoit, William L. and Dudley D. Cahn (1994). A Communication Approach to Everyday Argument. In Dudley D. Cahn (Ed.) *Conflict in Personal Relationships*, pp. 163-181 Hillsdale, New Jersey: Lawrence Erlbaum Publishers.

Braithwaite, Charles (1997). Blood Money: The Routine Violation of Conversational Rules. *Communication Reports* 10 (1), 63-73.

Burleson, Brant R., Terrance L. Albrecht and Irwin G. Sarason (1994). *Communication of social support*. Thousand Oaks, California: SAGE.

Daly, John A., Carol A. Diesel and David Weber (1994). Conversational Dilemmas. In William R. Cupach and Brian H. Spitzberg (Eds.), *The Dark Side of Interpersonal Communication*, pp. 127-158, Hillsdale, New Jersey: Lawrence Erlbaum.

Garner, Alan (1981). *Conversationally Speaking: Tested New Ways to Increase Your Personal and Social Effectiveness*. New York: McGraw-Hill.

Gottman, John M. (1994). The four horsemen of the apocalypse: Warning signs. In *Why Marriages Succeed or Fail*, pp. 68-102, New York: Simon & Schuster. (Topics: criticism, contempt, defensiveness, stonewalling).

Gottman, John M. (1994). The four keys to improving your marriage. In *Why Marriages Succeed or Fail*, pp. 173-201, New York: Simon & Schuster. (Topics: calm down, speak nondefensively, validation, overlearning-try and try again).

Markman, Howard, Scott Stanley and Susan Blumberg (1996). Communicating Clearly and Safely: The Speaker-Listener Technique. In Kathleen M. Galvin, K.M. and Pamela Cooper (Eds.). *Making Connections: Readings in Relational Communication*, pp. 197-205, Los Angeles: Roxbury Publishing.

Nofsinger, Robert E. (1991). *Everyday Conversation*. Newbury Park, California: SAGE.

Tannen, Deborah (1986). *That's Not What I Meant! How Conversational Style Makes or Breaks Your Relations With Others*. New York: William Morrow.

Tannen, Deborah (1990). *You Just Don't Understand: Women and Men in Conversation*. New York: Ballantine Books.

Rent

SEXUAL HARASSMENT

"RENT"

Tara knocks at Tom's door.

TOM
Come on in. Door's open.

TARA
Hi. Mr. Jewell, can I talk to you.

TOM
Mr. Jewell? That sounds so formal. I'm just your landlord. "Mr. Jewell" makes me sound like a high-school principal. Call me Tom.

TARA
Sure.

TOM
Sit down. Make yourself comfortable, etc. You know, I've never understood that word have you? "Etc." Why I ask the world but the world doesn't answer back. Do you want something to drink?

TARA
No. I'm fine thanks. I . . .

TOM
I have burgundy wine -- that's your favorite right?

TARA
Excuse me?

TOM
Well, there are always those bottles of burgundy wine in your trash.

TARA
I don't drink on weekdays.

TOM
Oh, come on, what a lame rule.

TARA
No, really. I have such a hard time getting up in the morning after I drink the night before.

TOM
One drink. Just so I won't feel so bad for having one.

                                    TARA

I really can't. But thanks. I appreciate it.

                                    TOM

For me. For putting in that new security door, huh? Besides -- you look nervous. Wine always helps calm me down. Have you had dinner? 'Cause I was just about to make some dinner. Would you like to join me?

                                    TARA

I wouldn't want to intrude.

                                    TOM

Not at all. I hate eating alone, don't you? 'Course you're not alone very much.

                                    TARA

I'd really love to stay Tom, but . . . my mom's coming to pick me up later.

                                    TOM

It'll give us time to talk. You do want to talk about something, don't you?

                                    TARA

Actually I did, but you look busy. I can come back.

                                    TOM

I'm not busy. Why don't you have some more wine. There's plenty here.

                                    TARA

One's my limit.

                                    TOM

Right. So what did you want to talk about?

                                    TARA

Rent.

                                    TOM

It is the first, isn't it.

                                    TARA

Yes it is.

                                    TOM

And you're supposed to pay me on the first, right?

                                    TARA

Yeah.

TOM

And your lease says if you don't you could be evicted, right?

TARA

Yes.

TOM

Boy, that's tough. You're not a vegetarian are you?

TARA

Excuse me?

TOM

Are you a vegetarian?

TARA

I could have sworn you said something else.

TOM

What?

TARA

Well, I thought you were asking me if I was a virgin.

TOM

Oh boy -- you have a naughty little mind, don't you?! I would never ask you a question like that! I might like to find out but . . .

TARA

I'm not . . . a vegetarian.

TOM

That's good. 'Cause the woman who lived here before you was. I'm always a little suspect of vegetarians.

TARA

Why?

TOM

They are so self-righteous. They think they've made such a superior choice. They act all natural. It's not natural. Men are hunters. It's in our nature to eat meat. You know, I like to think of myself as a nice guy, and I know times are tough.

TARA

You are -- a very nice guy. Dave and I have always thought so. You're a very nice landlord.

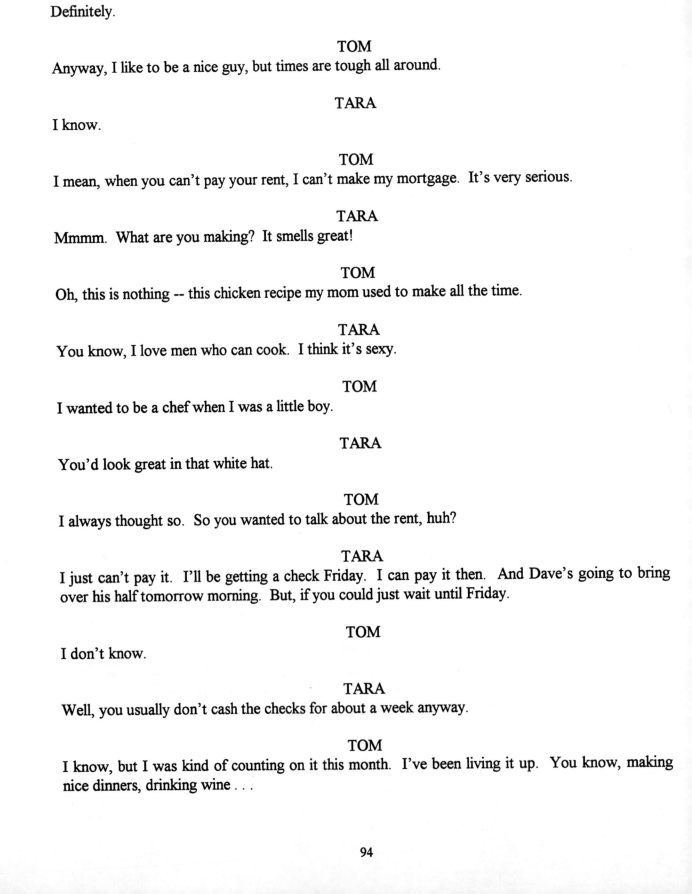

                              TOM

You really think so?

                              TARA

Definitely.

                              TOM

Anyway, I like to be a nice guy, but times are tough all around.

                              TARA

I know.

                              TOM

I mean, when you can't pay your rent, I can't make my mortgage. It's very serious.

                              TARA

Mmmm. What are you making? It smells great!

                              TOM

Oh, this is nothing -- this chicken recipe my mom used to make all the time.

                              TARA

You know, I love men who can cook. I think it's sexy.

                              TOM

I wanted to be a chef when I was a little boy.

                              TARA

You'd look great in that white hat.

                              TOM

I always thought so. So you wanted to talk about the rent, huh?

                              TARA

I just can't pay it. I'll be getting a check Friday. I can pay it then. And Dave's going to bring over his half tomorrow morning. But, if you could just wait until Friday.

                              TOM

I don't know.

                              TARA

Well, you usually don't cash the checks for about a week anyway.

                              TOM

I know, but I was kind of counting on it this month. I've been living it up. You know, making nice dinners, drinking wine . . .

TARA

Oh, I . . .

TOM

Don't be like that. There's no point in having money to spend if there's no one to share it with.

TARA

I'm sorry, Tom. But I really don't have the money. I don't know what else to say.

TOM

I guess we'll just have to work something out.

TARA

So we can . . . work something out?

TOM

If we can agree are on a reasonable payment plan.

TARA

Like a late fee or something like that?

TOM

Something like that.

TARA

That would be great. Dave would be so mad if I got us kicked out.

TOM

Yeah, it'd be pretty terrible if Dave didn't have a place to live because you failed to live up to your responsibility.

TARA

Yeah, I'd feel awful.

TOM

Thank the Lord for your looks, right?

TARA

What?

TOM

I was just thinking. It must be nice to have something to fall back on. I mean if you can't balance your checkbook, it's nice to have a safety net, right?

TARA

I can balance my checkbook, thank you very much.

TOM

Whatever. You can't pay the rent and it must be nice at times like this to have an option.

TARA

An option? What's my option?

TOM

You know what I'm talking about.

TARA

No, I don't think I do. You said we'd work something out.

TOM

"You'd look great in the big, white chef's hat," -- "Can we work something out?"

TARA

What?

TOM

Don't play dumb. You know what you're doing.

TARA

What are you implying?

TOM

You don't have to deny it. I don't care. In fact, I kind of respect a gal who can capitalize on her assets. That's fine with me.

TARA

I don't know what you thought I was thinking. But I wasn't, and I wouldn't.

TOM

Calm down. I'm not going to tell anybody -- unless we can't work something out -- but I thought we had worked something out.

TARA

But we haven't worked anything out.

TOM

Oh, so you'll have the rent tomorrow morning?

TARA

Tom -- I told you. I don't have any money.

TOM

That's a serious problem, isn't it?

TARA

I guess so.

96

                              TOM
Don't go getting self-righteous now. It's natural – it's a natural part of the barter system.

                              TARA
Prostitution?

                              TOM
What?

                              TARA
That's what you're talking about, right?

                              TOM
Where did you get that idea?

                              TARA
You just said . . .

                              TOM
Are you offering? Tara, I just wanted to have dinner.

                              TARA
I think I really need to go home.

Dave knocks on the door.
                              TOM
Come in.

                              DAVE
Rent. Hey, listen Tara. Plan B worked. My dad loaned us the rest of money for the rent . . . and something smells really good in here. I'm so hungry.

                              TARA
It's a chicken recipe from Tom's mom. Tom doesn't like to eat alone. Enjoy.

She exits.

                              DAVE
Can I sit down?

                              TOM
Sit down.

DAVE

Mmmmm. I haven't eaten all day. I wanted to thank you for putting in that new security door. I appreciate it.

TOM

What can I say -- I try to be a nice landlord.

-END OF SCENE-

"RENT"—SEXUAL HARASSMENT

Related Concepts in *THE INTERPERSONAL COMMUNICATION BOOK*

Primary Concepts: Unit 19: Power in Interpersonal Relationships

Power in Interpersonal Relationships
Principles of Power

Other Concepts: Unit 2: Axioms of Interpersonal Communication
                         Unit 8: Effectiveness in Interpersonal Communication
                         Unit 9: Universals of Verbal and Nonverbal Messages
                         Unit 13: Nonverbal Messages: Space and Time

Communication is Inevitable, Irreversible, and Unrepeatable
Interpersonal Communication is a Process of Adjustment
Interpersonal Communication is a Series of Punctuated Events.
Interpersonal Communications Have Content and Relationship Dimensions
Humanistic Model of Interpersonal Effectiveness
Pragmatic Model of Interpersonal Effectiveness
Meanings and Messages
     Meanings Are In People
     Meanings Are More Than Words and Gestures
     Meanings Are Both Denotative and Connotative
     Meanings Are Context-Based
Message Characteristics
     Messages Are Packaged
     Messages Vary in Directness
Spatial Messages

Questions about "Rent"

1. Did Tom's behavior amount to sexual harassment? Why or why not?

2. Was Tara sexually harassing Tom? Why or why not?

3. Tom never specifically asked for sexual favors. Is that relevant to whether sexual harassment took place?

4. The literature on sexual harassment usually refers to two types of sexual harassment: *quid pro quo*, where sexual favors are expected in exchange for something else, like a promotion or raise, or better grades; and *hostile atmosphere*, where the workplace or classroom is made uncomfortable or hostile because of unwanted references to sexual matters in a way that interferes with work performance. Which of these types of sexual harassment was present in this scenario?

5. Analyze the interaction between Tom and Tara according to the Bravo and Cassedy definition of sexual harassment.

6. Most of the articles about sexual harassment deal with a workplace or academic environment. Since Tom is not Tara's boss or her professor, can it be fairly said that he is capable of sexually harassing Tara? Why or why not?

7. Was Tom's behavior harmless? Why or why not?

8. Should Tara have simply ignored Tom's behavior? Should she have responded as she did? If not, how should she have responded?

9. Did Tara invite Tom to make sexual advances when she made the comments about being a vegetarian and/or when she made the comment about men who cook being sexy or that he would look good in a big white chef's hat?

10. Did Tara encourage Tom to continue making sexual suggestions by not confronting him earlier than she did?

Other Questions About Sexual Harassment

Memory Van Hyning suggested the following questions to help you determine whether sexual harassment has taken place. Analyze Tom's behavior according to these questions:
1. Was it real?
2. Was it related to their business?
3. Was it rejected?
4. Was it persistent?

Exercise 1: Practice Saying "No!"

In small groups, make a list of different types of unwanted sexual overtures students have encountered or heard of. From the list, each member of the group should choose two overtures that are particularly difficult to respond to. Working in pairs, have each member of the group role play how they would reject such overtures by having one group member act as the harasser and the other as the harassed. Have other members of the group evaluate the practiced behavior.

Exercise 2: Sexual Harassment Resources on the Web

Most colleges and universities have explicit sexual harassment policies. Look up the sexual harassment policy of your school and compare it to the policies of other schools, which can be found on most search engines by searching the term, "sexual harassment."

Additional Resources

Have students locate one or more of the following web sites and report what they learn to the rest of the class:

Sexual Harassment—Fact v. Myth   **http://www.vix.com/men/harass/myth.html**

Sexual Harassment: What Every Working Woman Needs to Know
http://www.cs.utk.edu/~bartley/other/9to5.html

Sexual Harassment essay by Dershowitz
http://www/vix.com/men/harass/dershowitz.html

Sexual Harassment Laws Become Tools of Censors
http://www.vix.com/men/harass.commentary/censor-tool.html

Sexual Harassment and Academic Freedom
http://www.nas.org/statements/harass.htm

Other References on Sexual Harassment

Barr, Paula A. (1993). Perceptions of Sexual Harassment. *Sociological Inquiry* 63 (Fall):460-471.

Bingham, Shereer G. (1991). Communication Strategies for Managing Sexual Harassment in Organizations: Understanding Message Options and Their Effects. *Journal of Applied Communication Research* 19 (June):88-115.

Buss, David M., and Neil M. Malamuth. (1996). *Sex, Power, Conflict: Evolutionary and Feminist Perspectives.* New York: Oxford University Press.

Clair, Robin P. (1996). Narrative Approaches to Raising Consciousness About Sexual Harassment: From Research to Pedagogy and Back Again. By Robin P. Clair, Pamela A. Chapman, and Adrianne W. Kunkel. *Journal of Applied Communication Research* 24 (Nov.):241-260.

(Commentary). (1992). Why Women Don't Quit Jobs When They Are Sexually Harassed. *Off Our Backs* 22 (Jan.):5.

Feary, Vaughana M. (1994). Sexual Harassment: Why the Corporate World Still Doesn't "Get It." *Journal of Business Ethics* 13 (Aug.):649-663.

Ivy, Diana K. and Stephen Hamlet. (1996). College Students and Sexual Dynamics: Two Studies of Peer Sexual Harassment. *Communication Education* 45 (April):149-166.

Kreps, Gary L. (1993). *Sexual Harassment: Communication Implications.* Annandale, Va.: Speech Communication Association.

Levy, Anne and Michele Paludi. (1997). *Workplace Sexual Harassment.* Upper Saddle River, N.J.: Prentice Hall.

Lipman, Elinor (1991). Are You the Office Sex Pest? Re-Educating the Guy Who Winks, Blinks and Smirks. *New York Times* 141 (Nov. 23):15(N), 23(L).

Mongeau, Paul A. and Jennifer Blalock. (1994). Student Evaluations of Instructor Immediacy and Sexually Harassing Behavior: An Experimental Investigation. *Journal of Applied Communication Research* 22 (Aug.):256-273.

Paetzgold, Ramona L. and Bill Shaw. (1994). A Postmodern Feminist View of "Reasonableness" in Hostile Environment Sexual Harassment. *Journal of Business Ethics* 13 (Sept.):681-692.

Paludi, Michelle, ed. (1996). *Sexual Harassment On College Campuses: Abusing the Ivory Tower.* New York: State University of New York Press.

(Panel Discussion). (1994). The Politics of Empowerment: A Paradigm Shift in Thought and Action For Feminists; New Questions Beyond the Feminist Focus on Sexual Harassment: Is It Helping Us Move From Victimhood to Empowerment, or is it a Diversion? *American Behavioral Scientist* 37 (Aug.):1122-1138.

Ring, Laura. (1994). Sexual Harassment and the Production of Gender. *Differences: A Journal of Feminist Cultural Studies* 6 (Spring):129-167.

Sharpe, Patricia., and Frances E.. Mascia-Lees. (1993). "Always Believe the Victim," Innocent Until Proven Guilty," "There is No Truth": The Competing Claims of Feminism, Humanism, and Postmodernism in Interpreting Charges of Harassment in the Academy. *Anthropological Quarterly* 66 (April):87-99.

Strine, Mary S. (1992). Understanding "How Things Work": Sexual Harassment and Academic Culture. (Telling Our Stories: Sexual Harassment in the Communication Discipline). *Journal of Applied Communication Research* 20 (Nov.):391-401.

Wood, Julia T., ed. (1996). *Gendered Relationships*. Mountain View, Calif.: Mayfield.

Wood, Julia T. (1992). Telling Our Stories: Narratives as a Basis for Theorizing Sexual Harassment. (Telling Our Stories: Sexual Harassment in the Communication Discipline). *Journal of Applied Communication Research* 20 (Nov.):349-363.

One More Chance

DYSFUNCTIONAL

RELATIONSHIPS

"ONE MORE CHANCE"

A small apartment. JEREMIAH, a twenty-four year old who works at a hardware store, sits watching television. His girlfriend, EMILY, gets home and puts her backpack, etc. away.

EMILY
Hey. *(no response from Jeremiah)* How was your day? *(still no response)* You didn't do the dishes? What are you watching? *(and yet still no response)* Fine.

JEREMIAH
Where were you?

EMILY
I had rehearsal. I told you I'd be late.

JEREMIAH
You said you had rehearsal until ten. Do you know what time it is?

EMILY
Rehearsal ran late, sorry.

JEREMIAH
Do you know what time it is?

EMILY
No, what time is it?

JEREMIAH
It's almost midnight. You're telling me your rehearsal went two hours late?

EMILY
Well, I was at the theatre until about eleven, then I had coffee with Amy.

JEREMIAH
Oh, you went out with Amy, huh?

EMILY
Yeah.

JEREMIAH
I've been waiting for you for two hours!

EMILY
I'm sorry. I just had coffee for half an hour. I didn't think it would be that big of a deal. I'm sorry.

JEREMIAH

No you're not or you wouldn't have done it.

EMILY

It's no big deal Jeremiah, calm down.

JEREMIAH

I hate Amy.

EMILY

So? So because you don't like her I can't see her? That's ridiculous.

JEREMIAH

That's not what I said.

EMILY

That's what you meant. That's what you always mean. I mean the fact -- the fact that you are so mad I was late, mad I was with her. You can't handle not having complete control over me. It's insane. We have this fight all of the time and you always say you'll work on it.

JEREMIAH

Didn't you think it would hurt me that you went out with her? I've been waiting for you for the last fifteen hours! But as soon as you have free time you go spend it with Amy?

EMILY

A half an hour Jeremiah.

JEREMIAH

Don't say my name like that! You sound like you're my mother or something.

EMILY

I'm sorry.

JEREMIAH

I've waited all day to see you.

EMILY

Well, that isn't my fault.

JEREMIAH

Of course it is. You're gone all the time!

EMILY

I'm gone doing things that are important to me. Do you understand that? School is important to me and theatre is the most important thing in my life. I mean why can't you understand that I have to do these things?

JEREMIAH

You are all I have!

EMILY

Well, I can't be what you want. We can't do this anymore.

JEREMIAH

What? Are you breaking up with me?

EMILY

Jeremiah . . .

JEREMIAH

Didn't I tell you not to say my name like that?

EMILY

I can't live like this anymore. Walking on eggshells, afraid that anything I say might set you off.

JEREMIAH

Look, I just want you to be a little more considerate of my feelings, that's all.

EMILY

But that's not all. You want me to think about you before I do or say anything.

JEREMIAH

Why shouldn't you?

EMILY

Because that's not right. I can't give you that much.

JEREMIAH

I've learned to put up with a lot from you. Why can't you cut me a little slack?

EMILY

What? First of all, if you can't put up with me then why do you want to be with me? And second of all, I have cut you plenty of slack!

JEREMIAH

How?

EMILY

What?! Do you not remember anything that happened two weeks ago? The black eyes and beating my head into the ground?

JEREMIAH

You say that like you didn't even do anything wrong!

Don't you even try to justify that! You can't justify that!

JEREMIAH

I'm not trying to justify it!

EMILY

Of course you are!

JEREMIAH

You did a terrible thing.

EMILY

I made a mistake and you need to get over it.

(Jeremiah shoves her against the couch)

JEREMIAH

Why don't you understand? Why do you do this to me? I've been trying so hard to make this work, and you don't do a damn thing to try and change things!

EMILY

I'm calling the police. *(she gets to the phone and begins to dial)*.

JEREMIAH

Emily, you can't do that.

EMILY

I'm not going to put up with this anymore.

JEREMIAH

I'm sorry.

EMILY

You're always sorry.

JEREMIAH

I'm just tired. *(by this time he has crossed to her and is holding her shoulders)* I'm a jerk, I'm sorry. Don't make me spend the night in jail. I love you.

EMILY

This is crazy Jeremiah. *(she hangs up the phone)*

JEREMIAH

I just freak out sometimes. I just can't deal.

EMILY

No. You need someone more . . . considerate, maybe? Someone who's willing to give up more and I guess I just can't handle things not going my way and I guess that's just how I am, you know?

JEREMIAH

No. I ask for too much.

EMILY

We're just not meant to be together.

JEREMIAH

Don't say that. Please. I don't know what I would do without you. You're the most important person in my life.

EMILY

But you need to change that. I will never be able to make you happy.

JEREMIAH

I don't need to be happy. I just need you.

EMILY

Jeremiah, you need to get a grip. No, forget --forget that. I'm sorry. God, I'm going insane. I just -- I worry about this.

JEREMIAH

Don't. Just be with me.

EMILY

You're addicted to me. I love you more than anyone in my life and you are addicted to me. That is so depressing.

JEREMIAH

I do love you.

EMILY

You need to go through withdrawal.

JEREMIAH

I have. I hate it! I'm sorry, I'm trying really hard.

EMILY

But it's still wrong and it's scary.

JEREMIAH

It's getting better.

EMILY

I hate being with you and I hate being without you.

JEREMIAH

Do you still love me Emily?

EMILY

Yeah.

JEREMIAH

Then give me just one more chance, okay?

EMILY

One more chance.

-END OF SCENE-

"ONE MORE CHANCE" - DYSFUNCTIONAL RELATIONSHIPS

Related Concepts in *THE INTERPERSONAL COMMUNICATION BOOK*

Primary Concepts: Unit 19: Power in Interpersonal Relationships

Power in Relationships
Power plays and moves
Bases of power
Characteristics of verbal abuse
Effects of verbal abuse

Other Concepts: Unit 20: Conflict in Interpersonal Relationships
                          Unit 17: Relationship Deterioration

Responding to verbal abuse
Communication in addictive relationships
Below-the-belt fighting
Verbal aggressiveness
Patterns of relationship deterioration
Negative communication cycles

Questions about "One More Chance"

1. What are some signs of abusive verbal communication?

2. What interpersonal patterns of communication are associated with verbal abuse (lack of openness, empathy, supportiveness, positiveness and equality; attacks to the other person's concept of self)?

3. Why do you think it's difficult for many people to confront verbally abusive people?

4. If you find yourself or a friend in an addictive relationship, what are some things that you might do about the situation?

5. How would you describe the relationship between Jeremiah and Emily? What behaviors by each person signal verbal abuse? What behaviors by each person signal an addictive relationship?

6. What recommendations would you make to Emily and Jeremiah about how they communicate with each other?

7. How do you see power displayed by Emily and Jeremiah (types and bases of power, power plays)?

8. What types of conflict strategies do Emily and Jeremiah use?

9. How do you distinguish between verbal abuse and verbal aggressiveness?

10. Why do you think this scene is titled "One More Chance"? What implications do the concluding lines of this scene have for this relationship? Do you think there are gender differences in the tendency to hope that a troubled relationship will improve?

Exercise 1: Script Analysis

The interaction between Emily and Jeremiah has a variety of examples of principles of power, conflict, and relationship deterioration. Complete the chart here, citing examples to depict each of the principles as demonstrated by Jeremiah and/or Emily.

COMMUNICATION BEHAVIOR	JEREMIAH	EMILY
Communicating Power		
speaking power	_____	_____
nonverbal power	_____	_____
listening power	_____	_____
Power Bases		
referent	_____	_____
legitimate	_____	_____
reward	_____	_____
coercive	_____	_____
expert	_____	_____
information/persuasion	_____	_____
Power Plays and Moves		
below-the-belt fighting	_____	_____
you owe me	_____	_____
nobody upstairs	_____	_____
Conflict Strategies		
avoiding	_____	_____
forcing	_____	_____
blaming	_____	_____
using silence	_____	_____
gunnysacking	_____	_____
face-detracting	_____	_____
Verbal Aggressiveness		
Aggressiveness	_____	_____
Abuse	_____	_____
Relationship Deterioration (Causes)		
unrealistic beliefs about relationships	_____	_____
excessive intimacy claims	_____	_____
third party relationships	_____	_____
relationship changes	_____	_____
undefined expectations	_____	_____
sex-related problems	_____	_____
work-related problems	_____	_____
financial difficulties	_____	_____

Exercise 2: Communicating through Scriptwriting and Acting

Divide the class in working groups of 3-5 students each. Select different segments of the script "One More Chance" that describe the interaction between Emily and Jeremiah. Provide each group with a copy of a different segment of the script. Each group's assignment is to rewrite its script segment <u>using effective communication strategies</u>. Groups then practice their scripts and perform/enact their scene for the other groups. Follow each performance with a class discussion about the changes made, the effectiveness and perceived authenticity, and the ease or difficulty of the actual communication portrayed in each scene.

Additional Resources

Films: *The Breakfast Club, Who's Afraid of Virginia Woolf?, Reality Bites*

The relationship advice columns in local newspapers often may offer comments about decisions to continue or to end a relationship.

Articles in many women's magazines (*Cosmopolitan, Working Woman, Glamour, Ladies Home Journal, Ms.*) frequently discuss communication in relationships and suggestions for a healthy personal, social and work relationship.

Other References on Dysfunctional Relationships

Bugenthal, Daphne B. (1993). Communication in Abusive Relationships. *American Behavioral Scientist* 36 (Jan-Feb):288-308.

Canary, Daniel J., William R. Cupach and Susan J. Messman (1995). *Relationship Conflict.* Thousand Oaks, California: Sage Publications. (Topics include parent-child conflict and conflicts in friendships and in dating and marital relationships).

Cupach, William R. and Daniel J. Canary (1997). Violence in Intimate Relationships. In *Competence in Interpersonal Conflict*, pp. 174-201, New York: McGraw Hill Companies.

Cupach, William R. and Daniel J. Canary. (1997). Guidelines for Managing Interpersonal Conflict. In *Competence in Interpersonal Conflict*, pp. 237-245, New York: McGraw Hill Companies.

DeSteno, David A. and Peter Salovey (1994). Jealousy in Close Relationships: Multiple Perspectives on the Green-Ey'd Monster. In Ann L. Weber and John H. Harvey (Eds.), *Perspectives on Close Relationships*, pp. 217-242, Boston: Allyn & Bacon.

Gottman, John M. (1994). Marriage styles: The Good, the Bad and the Volatile, *Why Marriages Succeed or Fail*, pp. 32-67, New York: Simon & Schuster.

Lloyd, Sally A. and Beth C. Emery (1994). Physically Aggressive Conflict in Romantic Relationships. In Dudley D. Cahn (Ed.), *Conflict in Personal Relationships*, pp. 27-46, Hillsdale, New Jersey: Lawrence Erlbaum Publishers.

Prather, Hugh and Gayle. Prather (1988), "How to Resolve Issues Unmemorably," *A Book for Couples*. New York: Doubleday.

Reardon, Kathleen K. (1995). *They Don't Get It, Do They? Communication in the Workplace--Closing the Gap between Women and Men*. Boston: Little, Brown & Co.

Shaver, Phillip R. and Cindy Hazan (1994). Attachment. In Ann L. Weber and John H. Harvey (Eds.), *Perspectives on Close Relationships*, pp. 110-130, Boston: Allyn & Bacon.

Vangelisti, Anita L. (1994). Messages That Hurt. In William R. Cupach and Brian H. Spitzberg (Eds.). *The Dark Side of Interpersonal Communication*, pp. 53-82, Hillsdale, New Jersey: Lawrence Erlbaum.

White, Jacquelyn and Barrie Bondurant (1996). Gendered Violence in Intimate Relationships. In Julia T. Wood (Ed.), *Gendered Relationships*, pp. 197-210, Mountain View, California: Mayfield Publishing.